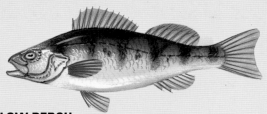

YELLOW PERCH

Length 5–12 inches, ½–2 pounds

The yellow perch prefers open water in large ponds, lakes, and clean, slow-flowing rivers. Yellow perch swim in schools, so several can be caught from the same area.

Length 12–20 inches, 1–5 pounds

Walleyes swim in schools in the deeper water of lakes and river channels, along the edge of weeds. They can be caught on various baits and lures.

MUSKELLUNGE

Length 18–40 inches, 2–30 pounds

The huge "muskie" is a spectacular fighter — and very difficult to catch. It lives in large rivers and lakes, ambushing its prey from the cover of submerged vegetation.

NORTHERN PIKE

Length 15–30 inches, 1–15 pounds

The pike is a voracious predator. In lakes, look for it in weedy bays and along reedy shorelines; in rivers, in the slower flow of shallow backwaters and downstream of islands.

LAKE TROUT

Length 12–20 inches, 1–15 pounds

Lake trout are found mainly in the Great Lakes and Canada. Although they prefer deep water, like most other fish they spawn in shallower water in spring.

BROOK TROUT

Length 5–24 inches, ¼–3 pounds

The little brook trout provides fine sport in cool, clear streams. Look for "brookies" and other river trout in deeper pools of water downstream of rocks.

RAINBOW TROUT

Length 12–21 inches, 1–15 pounds

Rainbow trout are found mainly in rivers but also in lakes. Some, called steelheads, migrate to the sea when young. Later they return to spawn in fresh water.

ATLANTIC SALMON

Length 12–36 inches, 2–20 pounds

An increasingly rare fish, the Atlantic salmon is found mainly in rivers. Very young fish go to the sea, later returning upriver to spawn. There are also several species of Pacific salmon.

LAKE WHITEFISH

Length 10–24 inches, 1–5 pounds

The lake whitefish is found in northern waters. It is often caught by fly anglers and by ice fishermen.

AMERICAN SHAD

Length 12–24 inches, 2–5 pounds

In spring, American shad swim upriver from the sea to spawn. They provide great sport on light tackle. Look for them in river channels and pools.

HOBBY HANDBOOKS™

FISHING

TONY WHIELDON

RANDOM HOUSE · NEW YORK

ACKNOWLEDGMENTS

The publishers would like to thank Kenny Collings and the staff of the Kenny Collings Angling Centre, 114 Carshalton Road, Sutton, Surrey FM1 4RL, for their assistance and the loan of most of the equipment and baits for the studio photography; Farlow's of 5 Pall Mall, London SW1, for their assistance and the loan of the sea-fly reel; Roy Westood, Editor of IPC Magazines' *Angler's Mail* magazine, and Neil Pope, Editor of EMAP Consumer Magazines' *Improve Your Coarse Fishing* magazine, for their help with the photographs for this book; and the organizations and individuals that have supplied the photographs reproduced on the following pages:
Ardea, London/Ake Lindau 57 bottom left. Bruce Coleman Ltd/Hans Reinhard 48-49 bottom. Robert Harding Picture Library 21 bottom left. Trevor Housby 61 bottom left. *Improve Your Coarse Fishing* magazine 18 top, 42. Lefty Kreh/Hillstrom Stock Photo Inc 30 top, 75 bottom. Mike Millman Photo Services 24, 31, 52 bottom, 54 (Nigel Pinsent), 56 top and center. NHPA/Roger Tidman 57 bottom right. Tony Oswald/Hillstrom Stock Photo Inc 8 right, 15, 30-31, 51 bottom right, 69 bottom left, 71 bottom. Reed International Books Ltd 81. Ken Schultz 28. Tony Stone Photographic Library, London/Jerald Fish 65 top left. ZEFA Picture Library, London/R. Jureit 69 bottom right.

Illustrators:
David Ashby: 11, 17 (top) 20, 21, 23, 24, 25, 27, 29, 34, 35, 36, 39, 40, 41, 43, 44, 45, 47 (top), 49, 50, 51, 52, 53, 55, 57, 58-59 (top), 59 (top), 60, 64, 66, 67, 68, 75.
Peter Bull Art Studio: 13, 15, 16-17 (bottom), 18, 19, 31, 32-33, 46 (top), 46-47 (bottom), 48, 58-59 (bottom), 65, 69, 71, 73.

Editor: Andrew Farrow
Series Designer: Anne Sharples
Designer: Mark Summersby
Picture Researcher: Liz Fowler
Production Controller: Linda Spillane

First American edition, 1994

Library of Congress Cataloging in Publication Data
Whieldon, Tony.
Fishing / Tony Whieldon ; [illustrators, David Ashby, Peter Bull Art Studio]. – 1st American ed.
p.   cm. – (Hobby handbooks)
Includes index.
Summary: Introduces the hobby of fresh and saltwater fishing, including the history of fishing, techniques of using baits and tackle, and safety tips.
ISBN 0-679-83442-7
1. Fishing—Juvenile literature. [1. Fishing.]   I. Ashby, David, ill.
II. Peter Bull Art Studio.   III. Title.   IV. Series.
SH441.W49   1994
799.1'2—dc20   93–22781

CONTENTS

Fishing as a Sport 8
Freshwater Rods and Reels 10
Line, Hooks, and Knots 12
Other Equipment 14
At the Water 16
How to Cast 18
Float Fishing on Still Water 20
Float Fishing on Rivers 24
Bites 28
Landing and Handling 30
Baits 34
Terminal Tackle 38
Pole Fishing 42
Fishing for Predators 46
Spinners, Spoons, and Plugs 50
Surf Casting 52
More at the Seashore 54
Boat Fishing 58
Sea-fishing Baits 62
Fly Fishing 64
Fly Fishing on Still Waters 68
Fly Fishing on Rivers 72
Saltwater Fly Fishing 74
Index 76

FISHING AS A SPORT

METHODS

This book introduces you to the many exciting methods of fishing. First some basic items of equipment are described. Then there are sections on float fishing for freshwater fish, landing and handling, baits, pole fishing, and fishing for predators. Next there's advice on fishing saltwater species from a boat or the shore. Finally there are sections on fly fishing for game fish, such as trout, sea trout, and salmon.

Fishing is mentioned in several old books, but it was not until the publication of Izaak Walton's *Compleat Angler* in 1653 that it was fully discussed as a sport. His little book, full of poetic verse and charming prose, praised angling as a sport and healthy recreation – and Izaak Walton lived to the ripe old age of 90! Today, there are millions of anglers worldwide.

An angler of Walton's time. The basket is called a "creel."

The great thrill of fishing is being out in the open air, using all your skill to hook and land a superb fish. Understand and appreciate your natural surroundings, and you will become a better angler.

spin-casting reel

JOIN A CLUB

There's lots to learn about fishing. Anyone starting from scratch should spend some time quietly watching experienced anglers using their local knowledge and "tricks of the trade." Join a fishing club. You can get the names and addresses of clubs in your area at your local tackle shop or library

SAFETY FIRST

Fishing can be great fun, but you must always be careful on or near the water. Always go fishing with an adult or companion, and don't fish near steep banks or slippery rocks. Find a flat, solid site. Tell another adult where you are going and when you will be back.

Some items of tackle are fun to look at and are works of art in their own right. This pike float, muskellunge spinner, and marabou fly-rod lure are just a few examples.

The spin-casting reel (below left) and the spinning reel (below right) are the types of reels most likely to be used by the beginner.

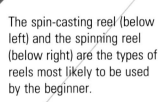

spinning reel

9

FRESHWATER RODS AND REELS

The huge variety of equipment available can be confusing for the beginner. Your local tackle dealer will be happy to help you. Start with the basics, a rod and reel. Unfortunately, no one rod is suitable for all types of fishing. Therefore, it is important to choose a rod that is right for the type of fishing you intend to do. The rods and reels shown here can be used for freshwater fishing on rivers and lakes.

SPIN-CASTING ROD

Spin-casting rods and reels are popular with beginners. They are simple to use and available in a wide price range. Buy a rod in a length that is comfortable for you to hold. (A 5½-ft to 6-ft rod is a good size for a beginner.)

spin-casting rod

handle

line guides

SPINNING RODS

Spinning rods vary in length from 4 ft to 12 ft, and are usually made of fiberglass, graphite, or a mixture of the two. The most popular lengths for general freshwater and shallow saltwater fishing are 6½ ft and 7 ft. Spinning rods are classified in "test curves," which indicate the flexibility of the rod (normally between 1¼ lb and 2¾ lb). The ideal breaking strain (bs) of line to use with a rod is four times the test curve. Using too light a line with the rod will damage the line. It is safer to use a line a little on the heavy side. Therefore, the ideal and minimum breaking strain line with a 1½-lb test curve rod would be 6-lb, but 8-lb would be acceptable.

spinning rod designed to cope with large, heavy fish such as carp and pike

spinning rod

ANGLER'S HINT
Your reel will be subjected to a lot of wear and tear, especially the constant retrieving of lure fishing. Make sure it performs smoothly by cleaning and oiling it regularly.

HOW TO LOAD A REEL

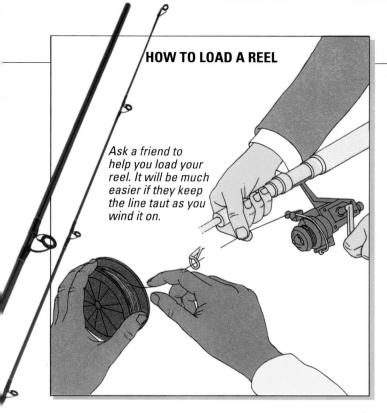

Ask a friend to help you load your reel. It will be much easier if they keep the line taut as you wind it on.

ROD ACTION

A fishing rod's flexibility is called its "action." Action is determined by the material, diameter, and taper of a rod. A tip-action rod has a flexible tip and is better suited to fishing for flounder (which has a delicate, not easily noticeable bite) than a stiffer, through-action rod, which is better suited to fishing for blackfish (which must be muscled off a rough bottom). When selecting a rod for yourself, consider the type of fish you are likely to catch, and ask for advice from local anglers or tackle dealers.

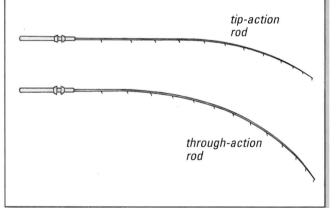

tip-action rod

through-action rod

SPINNING REELS

Spinning reels are suitable for most types of fishing on rivers and lakes. The line is held on a container called a spool, and it is wound in by way of a guide called a bale. Spools can be swapped using the release button on the front of the spool in the event you wish to quickly change to a different type or strength line.

SPIN-CASTING REELS

When casting into the wind with a spinning reel, the line will often blow back over the bale arm and create a tangle. This does not happen with the covered design of the spin-casting reel. For this reason, spin-casting, or closed-face, reels are ideal for float fishing into a wind. However, the flow of line is more restricted than from a spinning reel, which means more weight is needed to cast a particular distance. The restricted line flow can be an advantage when using stick floats (see page 26).

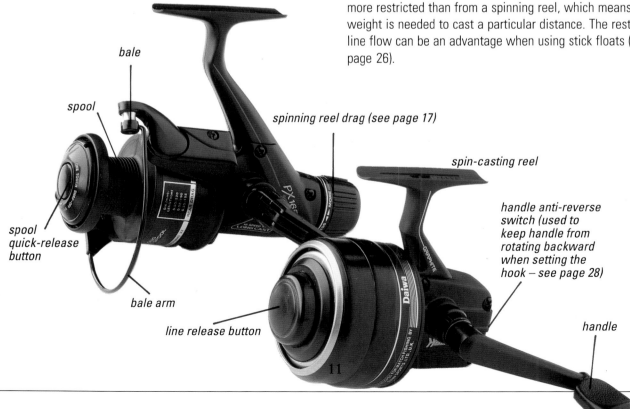

bale

spool

spinning reel drag (see page 17)

spin-casting reel

spool quick-release button

handle anti-reverse switch (used to keep handle from rotating backward when setting the hook – see page 28)

bale arm

line release button

handle

LINE, HOOKS, AND KNOTS

100-yd spool

Nylon monofilament line is available in 50-yd, 100-yd, or larger bulk spools. You'll need about 100 yd of line for loading freshwater reels. Bulk spools of more than 100 yd are used mostly by sea anglers.

bulk spool

Rods, reels, line, hooks, floats, and sinkers are known as tackle. Your tackle must be as light and inconspicuous as possible so that it doesn't frighten fish from the bait. On the other hand, it must be strong enough to hold the fish you want to catch! Fish will be more attracted to a neatly presented bait than one with odd strands of line all over the place.

LINE
A line of 2- to 3-lb "test" – the weight the line can hold without breaking – is suitable for float fishing; heavier 3- to 10-lb line is needed when using sinkers, or weights. Choose a line that is supple and doesn't stay coiled as it comes off the spool. This coiling is known as "memory," and means you will have less control of your float and hook.

HOOKS
The range of hooks is enormous. Saltwater and freshwater hooks can be bought loose or already tied to nylon: you will find it easier to start with hooks already tied to line. Check the knot on store-bought hooks connected to nylon before you use them – occasionally they are not tied or tightened properly.

Most hooks have a barb – a pointed part that projects backward from the hook's pointy tip. However, in many parts of the world it is becoming common practice to use barbless hooks. These hooks penetrate cleanly and can be removed easily, causing less damage to the fish. You can buy barbless hooks, or squeeze a barb with pliers so that it snaps off, leaving only a slight bump.

A leader is a length of line tied to the hook. A heavy leader is used when extra strength is needed to protect the line (from fishes' teeth, rocks, pilings, etc.). A lighter leader is used to make the line less visible to fish, enticing them to bite.

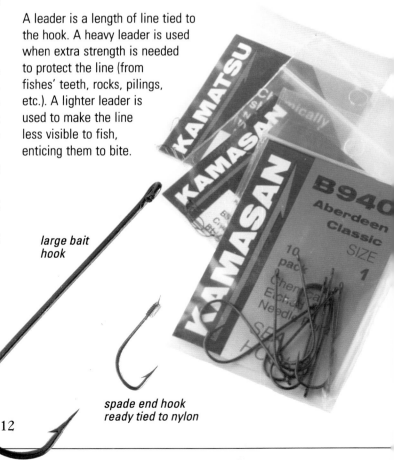

spade end hook *eyed hook*

barbless hook

barbed hook

large bait hook

spade end hook ready tied to nylon

12

KNOTS

It is important to be familiar with a selection of knots before you go fishing. First practice tying knots with a length or two of heavy line or string. Then practice tying them actual size, with the line you will be using.

pull

pull

DOUBLE LOOP KNOT
A useful knot for making a loop on the end of a line.

leader

LOOP-TO-LOOP ATTACHMENT
A useful and easily detachable method for connecting leaders to the main fishing line.

SPADE END KNOT
This knot gives a particularly neat presentation of the bait, especially with small hooks. It is well worth taking the time to master.

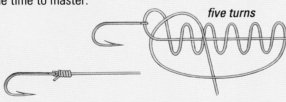

five turns

TUCKED HALF-BLOOD KNOT
This is probably the most widely used knot for attaching eyed hooks, leads, or swivels.

SLIDING STOP KNOT
This knot is tied on the main line when a sliding float is being used. It can be moved up or down the line to set the depth of the bait.

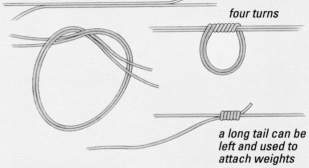

four turns

a long tail can be left and used to attach weights

WATER KNOT
This is a good knot for joining two lengths of line to each other.

DROPPER LOOP KNOT
Use the dropper loop knot to produce a connecting point for attaching various rigs as well as some lures, such as the redgill (see page 60).

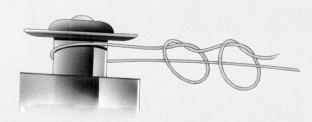

DOUBLE SLIP KNOT
Open the bale arm and use this knot to connect the main line to the reel.

ANGLER'S HINT
When tightening a knot into its final shape, ease it gently into position. Never jerk it hard, or you could damage the line. Moisten the knot just before tightening to make things slide into place more easily.

13

OTHER EQUIPMENT

Here is some equipment that you'll need for most forms of fishing. It's worth investing in good-quality, sturdy equipment that will stand the wear and tear of busy days by the water.

TACKLE BOX
A container for holding small items of tackle, the equipment an angler uses to catch fish — hooks, sinkers, lures, line.

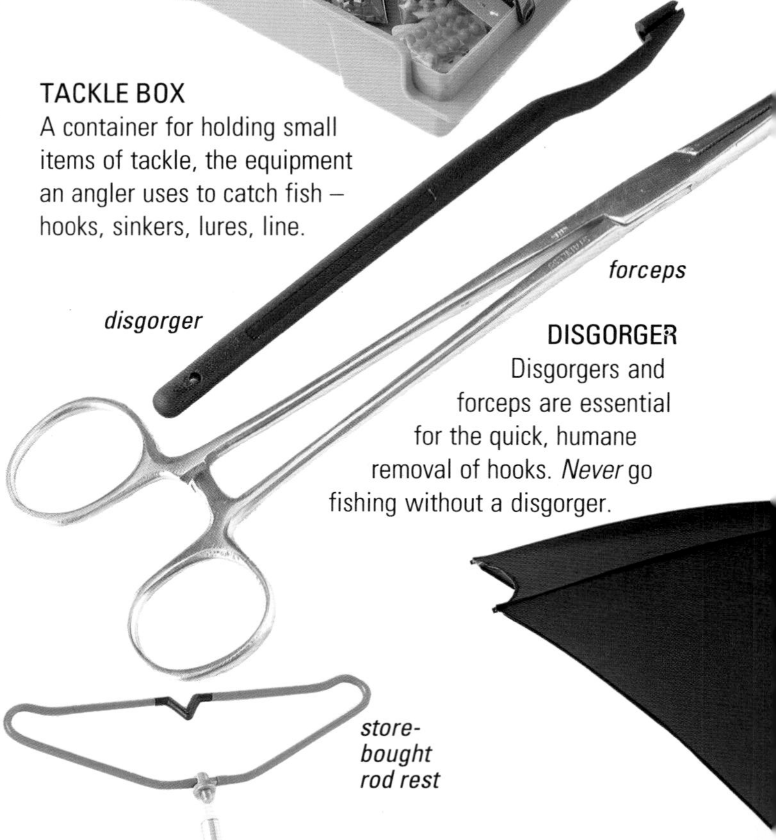

disgorger

forceps

DISGORGER
Disgorgers and forceps are essential for the quick, humane removal of hooks. *Never* go fishing without a disgorger.

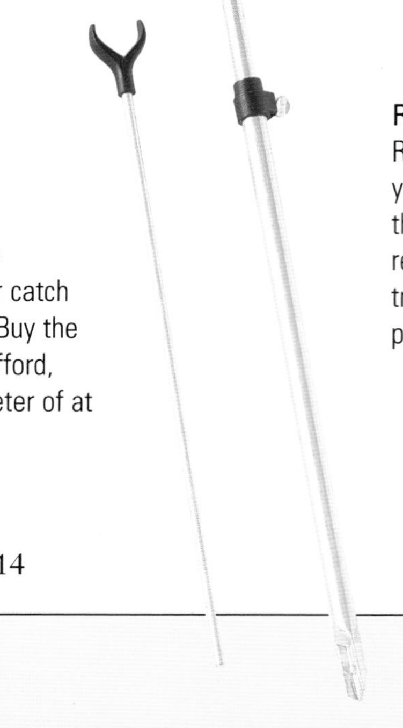

LANDING NET
A landing net is used to lift a hooked fish out of the water. This is a "pan" type landing net with a telescopic fiberglass handle. Many landing nets have a larger mesh.

store-bought rod rest

ROD RESTS
Rod rests can be used to hold your rod. Many different things can be used as rod rests (such as PVC piping or a tree branch), or one can be purchased at a tackle shop.

KEEPNET
Sometimes people use keepnets to hold their catch alive in the water. Buy the largest you can afford, with a ring diameter of at least 18 in.

USING ROD RESTS

right

wrong

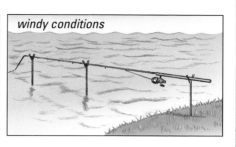
windy conditions

TOTEBAG
A bag can be very useful for carrying larger items of equipment, lunch, and extra clothes.

SPRING BALANCE
A spring balance is used to weigh catches of smaller fish or individual large fish.

SEAT BOX
This serves both as a seat and a container for items of tackle.

Wear sensible clothes to go fishing. Anglers find through painful experience that short sleeves and fishing do not go well together — biting insects thrive near the water. You may want to carry insect repellant in your tackle box.

UMBRELLA
An umbrella will shelter you and your tackle from rain, wind, and sun.

15

AT THE WATER

Before you can fish, you may need to buy a fishing license. A license, however, does not give you the right to fish anywhere – you still need permission to fish on private property. The owners of most waters will have their own rules, which should be on display. Carefully follow all the rules.

FISHING WATERS

The best way to get access to a good fishing spot is through a fishing club. If you don't have access to a club, check your library or newsstand for information on hot fishing spots. Many areas have local fishing magazines that give locations and information on types of fish present, popular baits, and cost.

SETTING UP

When you have chosen your fishing site, assemble your rod away from the water's edge so you don't disturb the fish. If you are using a three-piece rod, connect the top two sections first. Make sure the line guides are in line before pushing the sections together. Fix the reel firmly in position, open the bale arm, and thread the line through the line guides, making sure not to miss any. Next attach your float and weights, tie a loop on the end of the main line, and connect the leader with a loop-to-loop attachment.

Now position your seat at the water's edge and place your gear so it is within easy reach.

When you arrive at the water, don't start fishing in the first place you find. Some spots will be more likely to attract fish to feed than others. Scout the area and look for signs of feeding activity. When you have found a promising place, set yourself up quietly – fish can detect vibrations from heavy footsteps. A keepnet can be set up now, before you start to fish.

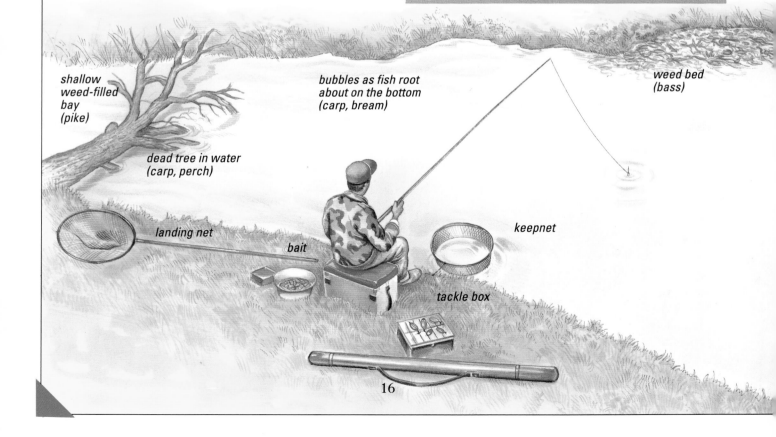

shallow weed-filled bay (pike)

dead tree in water (carp, perch)

bubbles as fish root about on the bottom (carp, bream)

weed bed (bass)

landing net

bait

keepnet

tackle box

ROD ASSEMBLED FOR FLOAT FISHING

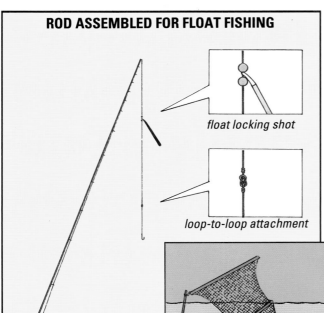

float locking shot

loop-to-loop attachment

SETTING THE DRAG

At the start of every fishing session, you must set, or adjust, the drag, a knob or screw-type device on your reel (see page 11). Setting the drag allows you to regulate how easily line will come off your spool when you've hooked a fish. Here's how: After threading the line through the rod guides, and before you tie on the hook, grip the end of the line with your free hand. Now lift the rod and flex the tip well over. Loosen (or tighten) the drag so that at this point it will release line grudgingly. Never tighten the drag completely, as this could result in the line snapping under the sharp pull of a big fish.

If the water is shallow, stake your keepnet out with a stick to keep it from falling flat.

fry scattering (pike or perch)

islands with overhanging trees (carp)

fish on the surface of their feeding area (trout)

lily pads (bass)

17

WARNING
CARBON FISHING RODS CONDUCT ELECTRICITY and ELECTRICITY KILLS.
Always fish away from overhead power lines.

HOW TO CAST

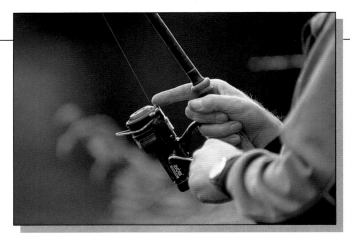

Casting is all about getting your bait out to the fish with the least disturbance. It is not difficult but requires practice and a correctly loaded reel. This section covers some basic casting techniques for fishing on lakes and rivers.

A correctly loaded reel, positioned well up the handle for good balance and control. The line should be loaded evenly, almost up to the spool's edge, and the reel should be within easy reach of your forefinger. Use as light a line as possible to achieve longer casts more easily.

CASTING

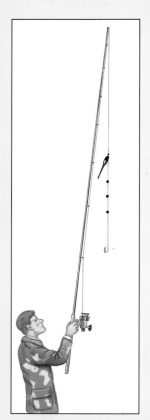

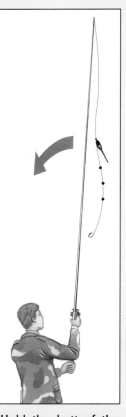

As the leader flies past the rod tip, at about 45°, release the line trapped by your forefinger.

Hold the rod up and out in front of you. Trap, or hold, the line against the handle with the tip of your forefinger and open the bale arm.

Hold the butt of the handle slightly away from you with your other hand. Lift the rod tip to just past the vertical.

Bring the rod forward with a smooth but positive action, keeping the butt in toward your body.

The line will spill rapidly from the spool as the tackle flies through the air. Follow through with the rod until it is about horizontal over the water. Re-engage the bale arm and wind in any slack (loose) line.

UNDERARM CAST

This is a simple cast for fishing close in to a riverbank. Trap the line with your rod-hand forefinger and open the bale arm. With your other hand, hold the line just above the hook.

Swing the rod up and out over the water, letting the hook go.

As the line flies past the rod tip, release the line at the reel. The hook and shot should land gently straight out in front of you.

Trap the line with your forefinger and close the bale arm.

HOW TO COMBAT A CROSSWIND

A wind blowing across you will have the effect of producing a bow, or curve, in the line as it flies through the air. This bow can be straightened out to some extent by feathering, or restraining, the line with the forefinger just before the tackle hits the water.

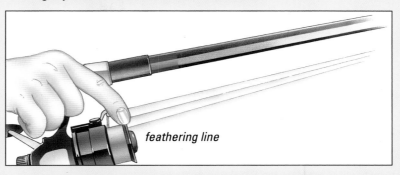

feathering line

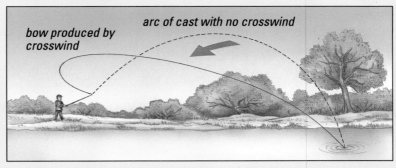

bow produced by crosswind

arc of cast with no crosswind

CASTING A SINKER

The basic method of casting also applies for casting a sinker, or weight (see page 38), although you should use a lazier action. The heavier tackle used will give a longer cast, but you will also get a larger wind bow in the line (see above) because there's more line airborne.

USING A MARKER

Accuracy is important. Try aiming at a feature on a far bank, such as a tree.

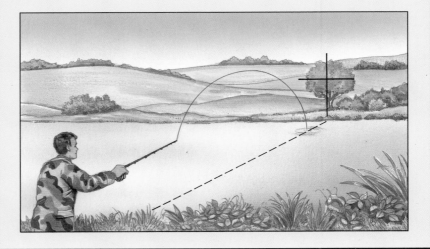

FLOAT FISHING ON STILL WATER

Float fishing uses a float to signal that a fish is taking your bait. For float fishing on still water, such as a lake or reservoir, you should set up your equipment and tackle as described on pages 16-17. You will now need to find the water's depth, using a heavy weight called a plummet, which is clipped onto the hook.

Floats for stillwater fishing, called quill floats, are made with a variety of materials including peacock quill, sarkandas reed and balsa wood. Some have a weighted base. This permits a longer cast while allowing light weights to be used farther down the line. When set correctly in the water, only the top of the float, the colored tip, should show above the surface.

PLUMBING THE DEPTH

Although a plummet may scare the fish in your spot, it will help you to place your bait on or near the bottom, where most fish feed. Estimate the depth of the water, and set the float at that depth. With the bale arm open and the line trapped by your forefinger, lob the plummet out in a smooth underarm swing, releasing the line as you would when casting. Leave the bale arm open until everything has settled and the float is hovering directly over the plummet. Reel in and, if necessary, adjust the position of the float until it stands at the correct depth in the water.

Now you can remove the plummet, bait your hook and cast out to catch some fish.

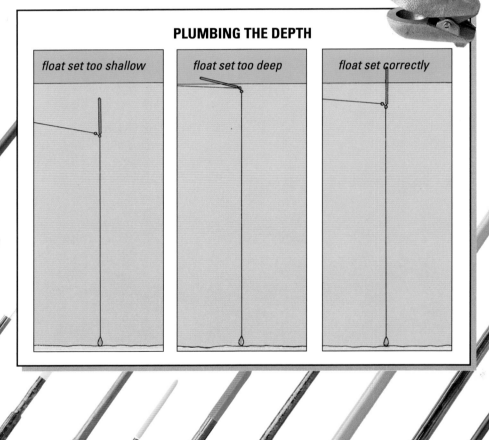

PLUMBING THE DEPTH

float set too shallow

float set too deep

float set correctly

FLOATS

For stillwater fishing, various types of floats can be used. The quill float below is attached to the line and locked in position by two or more small shot, or weights (see page 22). These "locking shot" also provide casting weight.

Quick-change float adaptors (above). Quill floats can be changed without having to reassemble your tackle.

Concentration is essential when float fishing, as the two young anglers (below) are demonstrating.

STILLWATER RIGS

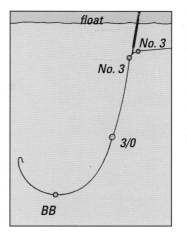

float
No. 3
No. 3
3/0
BB

This is a rig for fishing at close range or "on-the-drop." Because most of the shot (see page 22) is placed near the float, the bait falls slowly to the bottom. This may tempt fish that sometimes feed well off the bottom.

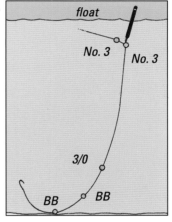

float
No. 3
No. 3
3/0
BB
BB

Use a rig like this when the surface of the water is drifting strongly. Placing heavier shot near the bottom of the rig helps to hold the bait down.

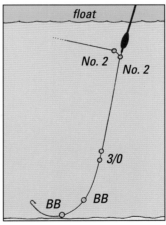

float
No. 2
No. 2
3/0
BB
BB

This rig has an arrangement of heavier shot for making longer casts and casts into the wind. The long, thin stem of this float is barely affected by surface drift on the water. This is a rig for deep water.

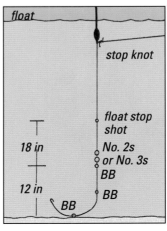

float
stop knot
float stop shot
18 in
No. 2s or No. 3s
BB
12 in
BB
BB

When fishing in very deep water, locking shot can't be used because the rig is too long to cast. Therefore a stop knot is used to stop the float at the correct depth, and the shot is "bulked," or arranged close together, farther down the line. A heavy shot load is needed for long casts into deep water.

21

SHOT

Shot is sometimes needed to cast floats and baits and to set floats correctly. It is available in a variety of sizes: the smaller the number, the bigger the shot. The larger sizes are used mostly as locking shot (to hold floats in position and to provide weight for casting), while smaller ones are spread down the line. If shot have to be bunched together – to combat surface drift, for example – they are referred to as bulk shot.

The amount of shot needed to set a float properly depends on the weather and water conditions. Shot should be squeezed firmly onto the line. Don't slide them along the line – it will damage the line. If you need to move shot after it is on your line, pry it open with your fingernail and reposition it.

Shot dispensers like this are simple to use. You can put shot back in for later use.

No. 2

No. 3

No. 2

No. 4

BB

No. 5

pliers

3/0

No. 7

SINKING THE LINE

The surface layer of water tends to move in the wind, creating a bow in the line and dragging the float out of the feed area (the place where the fish are biting). Avoid this problem by sinking the line beneath the surface, as shown below.

Cast some distance beyond the feed area.

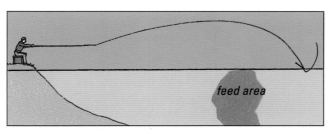

Sink the rod tip beneath the surface.

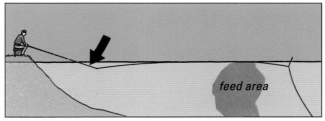

Reel in until the tackle is over the feed area.

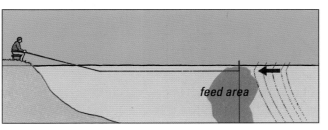

KEEPING A RECORD

Having found the depth of the water, keep a record of its depth for the next time you visit. (You may need to take into account seasonal variations in the water level.) There's no need to measure your line – just make a note of the number of rod line guides from the float to the hook. If the depth varies across a body of water, use features in the distance as a guide to direction – if you fish from the same spot you can use them as aiming points.

Why not keep a log book of all your outings? Note the day, time, exact location, and weather, and also the details of the tackle and baits you have success with. This will help you learn the best rigs, locations, and circumstances in which to fish. Stick in photos of your best catches!

It can be very useful – and enjoyable – to look back on a well-kept log of your previous fishing outings.

Location	Date	Hours	Weather	Catfish	Bass	Trout	Pike	Salmon	Bream	Carp	Perch	Notes
...ke ...onkonkoma ...across from ...ublic beach)	6/16 2pm	2	Warm but overcast, light breeze	1½lb +3							1lb	

FLOAT FISHING ON RIVERS

A good method of float fishing in moving water is called free spooling. The float is cast into the current and the bale arm is left open so that the line can be pulled from the spool. The float is then allowed to run downstream with the current, presenting the bait to the fish in as natural a way as possible.

READY TO FISH

There's no need to use a plummet to find the depth of a river. Instead, set the float at the estimated depth of the water and make a practice cast. If the float travels through the water freely, move it up the line and cast it downstream again. When the float falters occasionally on a run, or drift, that shows you have the correct setting, with the bait just off the bottom.

Although spinning reels can be used for float fishing, a spin-casting reel is more effective as it does not spill line so readily. If you are using a spinning reel when your bait is taken, trap the line with your finger, and lift back on the rod to "set the hook," i.e. to hook the fish. Immediately engage the bale arm with a quick turn of the handle, then play the fish (see pages 30-32).

CONTROLLING THE BAIT

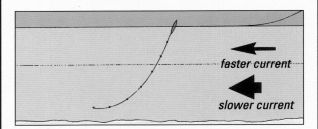

This is the correct arrangement of float tackle as it makes its way downstream, with the hookbait and shot always ahead of the float. Use your finger to trap the line slightly at the reel, so the hookbait precedes the float.

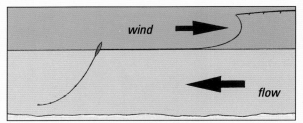

The ideal condition for free spooling is when the wind is blowing upstream. This holds back the float so that the hookbait precedes it downstream.

You'll have to watch and control your tackle constantly as it moves downstream. It is easiest to free spool when the fish are directly downstream of the rod tip. If the area you want your float to drift through is farther out than the length of your rod, lob the tackle out with a smooth underarm cast.

CONTROLLING THE FLOAT

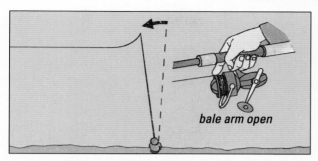

bale arm open

Follow the float with the rod tip, a fraction slower than the speed of the surface water, with your finger trapping the line.

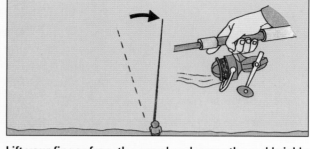

Lift your finger from the spool and move the rod briskly away from the float. Line will come off the reel. Retrap the line and repeat the procedure.

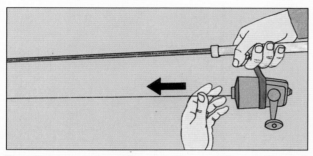

The slightly restricted line flow from a spin-casting reel makes it ideal for drifting a float. Some control of the line, using your free hand, may be needed occasionally.

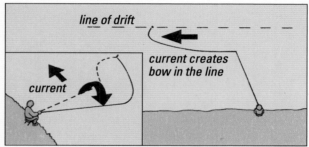

line of drift

current creates bow in the line

current

If the line of the drift is beyond the rod tip, the current may produce a bow in the line, dragging the float off course. This can be cured by trapping the line at the reel and simply lifting it over with the rod.

Bubble floats (below right) are used to provide casting weight for small, light baits. Some bubbles are transparent and excellent for stillwater fishing; others are brightly colored for good visibility.

Large-bodied hollow plastic floats (above) are very buoyant, or able to stay afloat. They are used to suspend heavy baits, such as deadbait (a piece of, or whole, dead fish used as bait), above the lake, river, or sea bottom. The float can be fixed in position if the water is less deep than the length of the rod. Or it can be restrained by a stop knot if the bait has to be very deep in the water (see page 21). The fluorescent floats pictured are visible in deep shadow (beneath overhanging trees, for example).

25

ANGLER'S HINT
After each drift downstream, the tackle should be retrieved *away* from the fishing area. If you pull the tackle through the fishing area, the fish may be frightened away.

FLOATS

Floats, or bobbers, are used to suspend bait in the water (for example, above an obstructed bottom where your hook might get snagged, or at the level in the water where the fish are biting), and also to indicate – with a bobbing motion – when a fish is biting. They are made of various materials that float, such as plastic, cork, and balsa wood.

STICK FLOATS

Stick floats are the lightweights of the river. They are ideal for fishing smooth, medium-paced water, about 4 ft deep.

PLASTIC BUBBLES

The plastic bubble is the most popular type of float in use today. It can be found in almost every tackle shop from coast to coast. The red and white color makes the bubble highly visible in the water, and its shape allows a longer cast than the stick or egg floats.

EGG FLOATS

Egg floats are a cross between stick floats and plastic bubbles. The bulging "egg" portion provides stability and buoyancy in rough water when a stick might be knocked over.

CORK BALLS

Cork balls are similar in shape and function to the plastic bubble but are made of cork. Both cork balls and plastic bubbles are used in salt and fresh water as general, all-purpose floats.

Line is run through the cork ball float and held in position with a stopper.

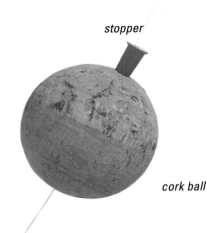

stopper

cork ball

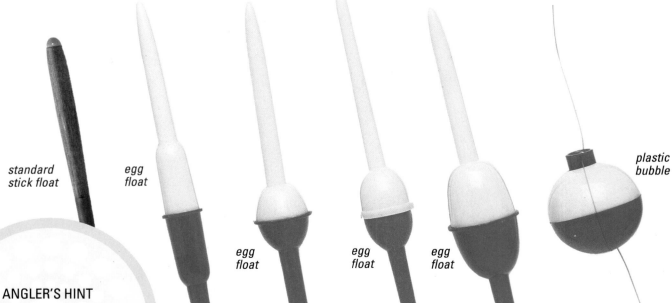

standard stick float

egg float

egg float

egg float

egg float

plastic bubble

ANGLER'S HINT
The easiest way to apply floatant to line is to spray it while the line is still on the reel spool.

SHOTTING PATTERNS

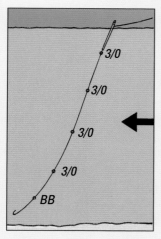
3/0
3/0
3/0
3/0
BB
flow

A stick-float rig with shot spread evenly down the line works well in slowly flowing water.

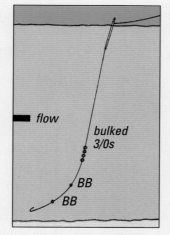
flow
bulked 3/0s
BB
BB

In slightly faster water it may be necessary to bulk the shot nearer the hook to keep the bait down.

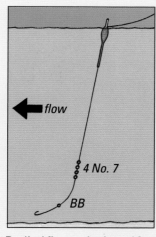
flow
4 No. 7
BB

Bodied floats, designed for fast-flowing water, are usually used with shot bulked well down the line.

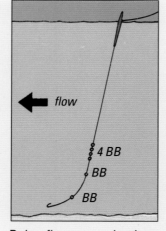
flow
4 BB
BB
BB

Balsa floats are also best used with the shotting bulked. They are a good alternative to stick floats when the water is running higher than normal.

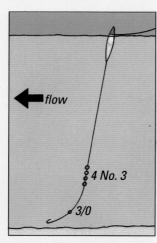
flow
4 No. 3
3/0

Some floats are buoyant and can carry a large amount of bulk shot in rough water conditions.

SNAGS

There's always a risk of snagging your line on an underwater obstruction. If you know the position of an obstruction, hold the float back harder than normal so that the hookbait will swing up and over the snag.

Having an intimate knowledge of an area certainly helps to avoid snags. Take a look at the water when it is running low and clear on a bright sunny day. Wear sunglasses, which cut out the surface glare and allow you to see objects more clearly under the water.

If it has been raining hard and the river level is high, try casting into slow-moving areas. Fish often move close to the bank to avoid excessively strong currents.

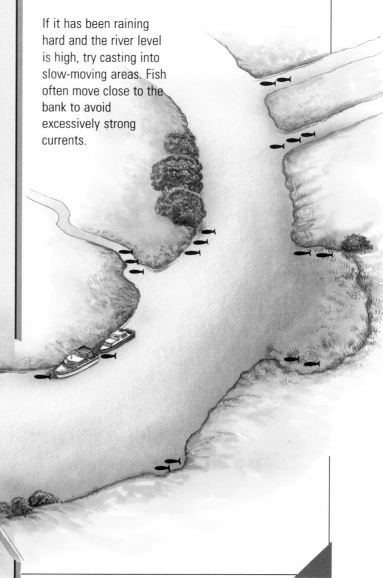

BITES

Bites indicate that fish are interested in your bait, but all fish bite differently. Some species feed in a delicate manner, sucking or mouthing the bait before eventually taking it more firmly. Others will grab it and run.

BITES ON FLOAT TACKLE

The movement of a float will often show what kind of fish is at the end of the line. If you can interpret these float signals, building up a mental picture of what is happening beneath the water, you will be able to respond at the right time and hook the fish in a proper manner.

SETTING THE HOOK

The point at which you lift the rod and hook the fish is known as setting the hook. You should set the hook firmly and without hesitation so that any slack in the line is taken up, but not so hard that the hook is ripped out of the fish's mouth.

A correctly hooked fish should have the point of the hook embedded in the mouth area, where it is easy to remove, either by hand or with a disgorger. A badly hooked fish (one which has taken the bait deep into its gullet) is usually the result of an inattentive angler. Therefore pay constant attention to the float while the bait is in the water. If you have to move away from the area, even for a few moments, wind in your tackle, and re-cast when you return.

A predator snapping at a spinner or plug (see page 50) will hook itself. Usually the hook or hooks will be caught in the front part of the jaw, as with this North American walleye. This means the fish can be unhooked cleanly and quickly.

BITES

LIFT BITE

This is a common type of bite when a bait is fished on the bottom.

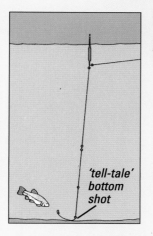

'tell-tale' bottom shot

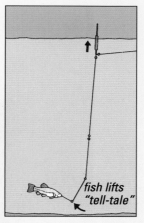

fish lifts "tell-tale"

The fish takes the bait and rises off the bottom, taking the bottom shot with it. The float rises immediately. Set the hook at this point to hook the fish cleanly.

A VARIETY OF BITES

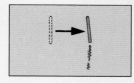

Sometimes the float will start to move along the surface. Set the hook immediately, in the opposite direction to the float movement.

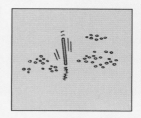

When fish are rooting on the bottom, the float will often dither and bob as fish bump into the bait. Don't set the hook until the float moves distinctly.

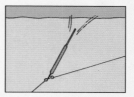

There is no mistaking this "sailaway" bite. Sometimes the float will dart underwater quickly; at others it will sink slowly – set the hook immediately!

PIKE AND BASS BITES

When pike or bass take a fish bait, the float moves away and under very positively. It used to be accepted practice to let the fish take the bait well into its mouth before setting the hook. This resulted in many deeply-hooked fish. Nowadays, thankfully, this practice is frowned upon; you should strike immediately to set the hook in the mouth area.

ON-THE-DROP BITE

After the cast, the float will settle lower and lower (see bottom diagram) as each shot settles into position. Any break in this sequence will probably mean that a fish has taken the bait. This is the time to set the hook.

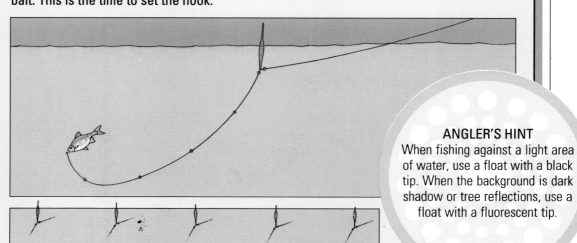

ANGLER'S HINT
When fishing against a light area of water, use a float with a black tip. When the background is dark shadow or tree reflections, use a float with a fluorescent tip.

LANDING AND HANDLING

It takes skill to land, or bring in, a large specimen. Imagine you are fishing a lake that contains large bass. Your reel is loaded with 4-lb test line, attached to a leader of 3 lb, which in turn is whipped to a size 14 hook baited with a single earthworm. Soon you see large swirls on the surface. The bass are moving in...

THE BATTLE BEGINS

Suddenly the float is gone. On lifting the rod to set the hook, you feel the solid resistance of a big fish – 5 lb at least! It is hooked and tries to escape. It makes a long run away from you, taking line off the spool against the resistance of the reel's drag. There's no doubt you've hooked a fighter!

You can't just reel it in, because it's too strong for your tackle. So you apply a little extra pressure to the spool with your forefinger. This restrains the line, causing the fish to change course – veering toward a large bed of water lilies! If it reaches them the line will snag in the stems, and the fish will be lost!

PLAYING THE FISH

So far you have been holding the rod well up, using its flexibility as a shock absorber. Now you must quickly lay the rod over to the left, finger still on the spool, in an attempt to turn the fish away from the snag. Under your skillful control, it veers away.

When the fish shows signs of tiring, "recover" line by lowering the rod toward the fish, winding in line as you do so. Use the rod as a lever to pull the fish toward you, then lower the rod again and wind in more line. Be prepared for the fish to get a second wind and make another long, powerful run. If the fish heads toward you, raise the rod high and wind in line quickly – the fish could come off the hook if the line goes slack.

HOW TO PLAY A FISH
Use a firm, steady pumping action to recover line. Always keep the rod tip high when playing a big fish.

Pull the rod up, using its action to gain line.

Let the rod out to the fish, winding in the gained line.

Repeat the process, easing back the rod to gain line.

Apply side strain to turn a fish away from a snag.

A critical time when playing a fish is when it is being drawn to the net (left). A fish will often find a reserve of energy and make a powerful run. If you are not prepared for this sudden surge, it could snap your line or pull the hook free.

To land very small fish, hold the rod at about 45° and reel in. When the length of line from the rod tip to the fish is the same as the rod, lift the fish from the water and swing it in to your hand. This young angler has wound in too much line.

INTO THE NET

After a spirited battle your fish tires and circles under the rod tip. You reach for the landing net. You hold the net still, the rim just beneath the surface, and bring the fish over it. You lift the rim of the net clear of the water, and claim your prize!

UNHOOKING

Once caught, the fish must be unhooked. Lay down your rod, and with both hands slide the net toward you. The fish should be perfectly hooked, just inside the top lip, so that a nudge with a disgorger will have the hook out in a second.

If you believe you have caught a record fish, find witnesses to your catch and take a photo of it. Write down all the details of the catch – time, location, weight of fish, how it was caught, and the names and addresses of any witnesses. Make sure the fish is weighed in at an official weigh-in station.

HOW TO HANDLE FISH

Wet your hands before handling a fish. This is because fish are covered in a coating of protective slime, which will stick to dry hands. If a fish loses this protective coating, it will be more susceptible to infection and disease.

Small fish can be held in the hand to have the hook removed. Larger fish should be laid on a soft, damp surface. Use pliers for removing hooks from sharp-toothed fish like pike.

Use a weighing sling when weighing your catch. Never weigh a fish by the gills if you intend to return it to the water.

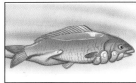

Hold large fish upright in the water until they can swim away of their own accord.

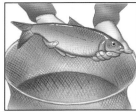

Place fish gently into a keepnet – do not drop them in. Never put too many fish in a keepnet.

Very large carp should never be kept in keepnets. Keepsacks are far better.

When releasing fish from a keepnet, hold the net and let the fish swim out.

UNHOOKING A PIKE

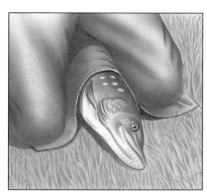

Be firm but gentle when unhooking large predators such as pike. Lay the fish on its side on a soft, damp base or on grass. Kneel astride but not on the fish. Wear a soft gardening-type glove on one hand.

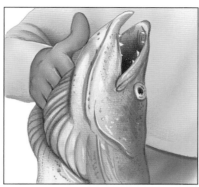

Now slide your gloved forefinger beneath the fish's gill cover and forward toward the front of the jaw. Lift the pike's head just off the ground and its mouth will open. A pike can also be carried like this.

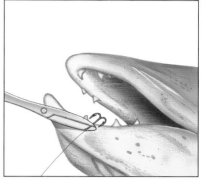

Use forceps or long-nosed pliers to remove the hooks, gripping them by their shanks. Small-barbed or barbless hooks are easiest to remove.

USING A DISGORGER
Keeping the line taut, slide the disgorger down the line until you feel the resistance of the hook. Give a slight push and the hook will come free. Don't use too much force. If you can't free a hook, cut the line as close to it as possible — the hook will probably rust away.

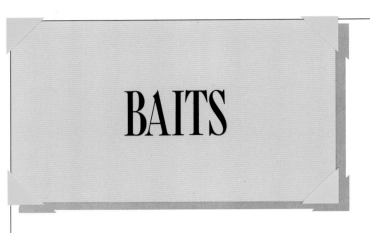

BAITS

There isn't one "magical" bait that will catch a fish on any occasion, so carry a selection in case your favorite one isn't working. The baits shown here are just a few used by anglers, and you can experiment with others. Many baits, such as maggots and nightcrawlers, can be bought from tackle shops.

MAGGOTS
Maggots are the soft legless larvae of certain flies. Large whites are the most widely used maggots. Pinkies and squatts are much smaller maggots that make good hookbait when fishing with very fine tackle. If you are not using them immediately, store maggots in a cool place.

Carefully thread maggot pupa (the inactive stage in a fly's life cycle between the larva and adult forms) onto a hook as shown. If the skin of the pupa is firm, thread the hook so that its point protrudes outside the pupa (which makes it easier to hook a fish).

hook buried

hook protruding

BREAD CRUST AND FLAKE
Bread crust is a buoyant bait, ideally suited to surface fishing for carp, or for fishing over a layer of bottom weed. Bread flake is an excellent bait for chub and carp.

large whites

squatts

pinkies

bread crust

PREPARING BREAD PASTE

Remove the crust from a stale sliced loaf of white bread.

Soak the slices in cold water until they are soggy but do not fall apart.

Wrap the slices in a clean cloth and squeeze them to remove excess water.

Knead the bread until it becomes a firm, smooth, but non-sticky paste.

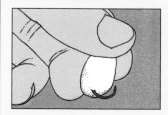

Carefully mold the paste around the hook, leaving the point exposed.

LUNCH MEAT

This is a convenient bait because it will keep almost indefinitely in an unopened can. Carp and chub love cubes of this tasty offering.

PUNCH AND PASTE

Bread punch is an ideal carp bait. It is named after the tool that is sometimes used to cut out a small piece from a slice of bread and transfer it to the hook. Paste is made by mixing bread with water. Some anglers flavor it with honey.

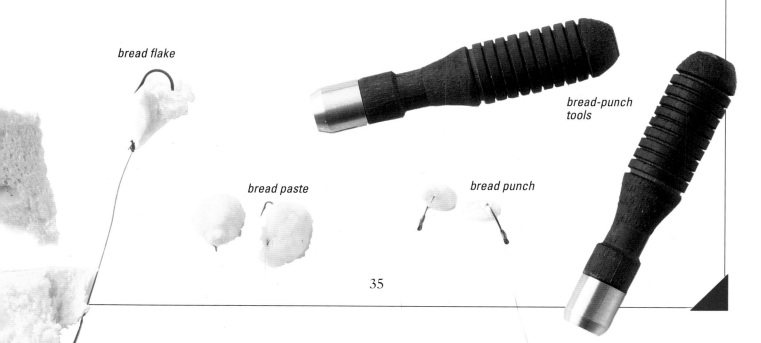

bread flake

bread paste

bread punch

bread-punch tools

GROUNDBAIT

When fishing for bottom-feeding fish, you might want to try to bring a fishing spot to life by introducing groundbait before you start. This European practice is similar to what is called "chumming" in the United States. In groundbaiting, a breadcrumb mixture is introduced to an area to attract fish. In chumming, ground-up bait – fish, shellfish, even dog food – called "chum" is added to the water to whet the fishes' appetites!

GROUNDBAIT

The basic ingredients in groundbait are breadcrumbs and water from the spot you're fishing. Pieces of hookbait can also be added to the mixture. Groundbait is rolled into balls and thrown by hand into the water. In some parts of the world, a groundbait catapult is also sometimes used, especially when fishing at longer ranges.

MIXING GROUNDBAIT

Mix groundbait at the waterside before you assemble your fishing gear. Add some river water to a generous amount of breadcrumbs. Knead well with both hands, adding more water if necessary, until the mix can be formed into balls.

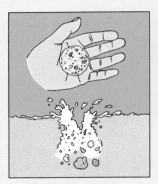

After you've set up your tackle, throw several golfball-sized groundbait balls into the area you intend to fish. The balls will break on impact.

It is worth groundbaiting a couple of areas – you can alternate between them as you fish. You should also keep some groundbait for use later in the day. Store it in a cool, shady position so it doesn't dry out.

groundbait catapult

nightcrawlers

NIGHTCRAWLERS

Nightcrawlers can grow very large, and make an ideal bait for carp and large perch. They can be collected from the surface of a damp lawn, after dark, when they emerge from their holes. Pop them into a ventilated container lined with damp moss where they will scour themselves clean. Don't put them in soil – they'll create a slimy mess.

redworms

REDWORMS

Redworms are lively worms that can be found in compost and well-rotted manure, or under leaf mold. Use small ones of about 1 in in length for sunfish, and 2 in ones for bream and bass. You can make your own redworm trap by placing a wet sack on damp, shaded ground.

BRANDLINGS

These are like redworms but have light body rings. They can be found in manure heaps. Unfortunately for anglers they have a very pungent smell, though this doesn't seem to bother the fish.

brandlings

CHEESE

Cheese should be considered a fun bait, one to experiment with when not much else is working. Try using it when fishing for carp.

CANNED CORN

Another fun bait to try when fishing for carp. Open the can at home and transfer the pieces to a plastic container.

TERMINAL TACKLE

Terminal tackle is a collective name given to anything attached to the end of your fishing line, such as sinkers, swivels, snaps, hooks, leaders, and lures. Tackle availability and usage varies from place to place.

SWIVELS
Swivels are often used to allow a bait or lure to move without spinning the line. Swivels are tied between the line and the leader.

SNAPS
Snaps are used to allow a sinker, weight, or lure to be changed rapidly. They work like safety pins and can be attached directly to the line or to a leader. Snap swivels are snaps with swivels attached, and they are used, like swivels, to prevent a line from spinning.

SINKERS
If the fish are feeding a long way out from the bank, or along the bottom, you may need to use a sinker to reach them. Sinkers come in a variety of shapes and sizes for use under various fishing conditions. They are usually made of lead and are tied or pinched onto a line. Sinkers can be used in both fresh- and saltwater fishing.

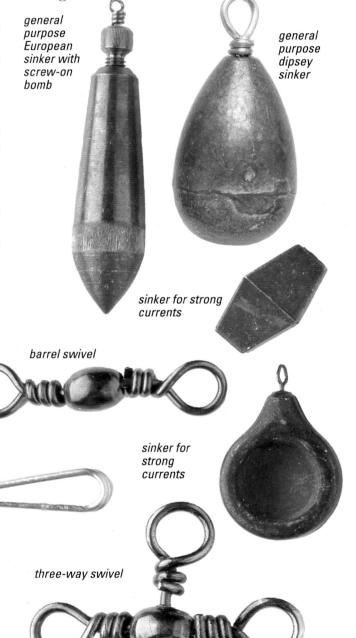

general purpose European sinker with screw-on bomb

general purpose dipsey sinker

sinker for strong currents

link swivel

barrel swivel

link swivel

sinker for strong currents

snap swivel

three-way swivel

38

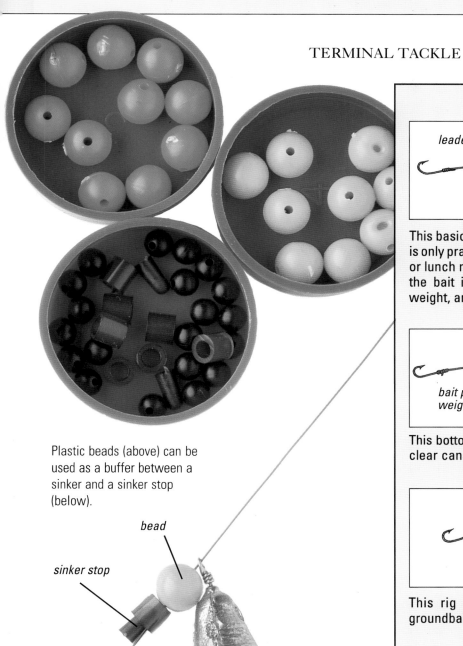

Plastic beads (above) can be used as a buffer between a sinker and a sinker stop (below).

bead

sinker stop

Sinker stops (above) are anchor points for weights. They are much kinder to the line than split shot and can be used time and time again. Keep a good supply in your box, though, because they are easily lost.

WEIGHTED RIGS

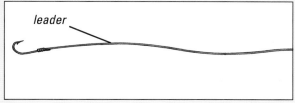

leader

This basic freeline bottom rig is very sensitive, but it is only practical with large baits such as bread paste or lunch meat. Large, wary carp, which would drop the bait if they felt the resistance of any added weight, are often fooled by a rig like this.

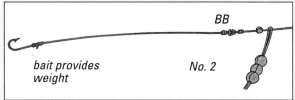

BB

bait provides weight

No. 2

This bottom rig is used for fishing at close range on clear canals and small rivers.

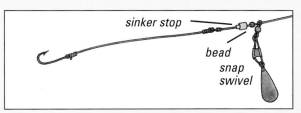

sinker stop

bead

snap swivel

This rig is a good basic system for fishing a groundbaited area.

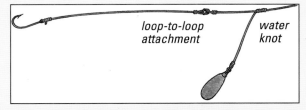

loop-to-loop attachment

water knot

The fixed link rig is a streamlined, sensitive rig designed to present the bait when there's a soft, silty lake bed. The sinker sinks into the silt but leaves the line exposed.

FEEDERS

If fish are not biting, you can try using something called a feeder to lay groundbait close to your hookbait. Feeders are stuffed with groundbait, maggots, or other chopped bait, and attached to your line with a snap swivel. They are cast into the water along with your hookbait. Once in the water the groundbait mix crumbles away, tempting fish to investigate the scene.

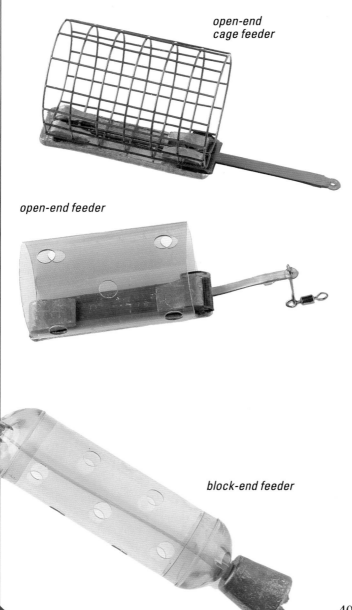

open-end cage feeder

open-end feeder

block-end feeder

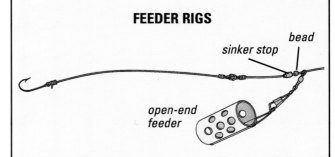

FEEDER RIGS

bead
sinker stop
open-end feeder

The open-end feeder rig is a favorite for laying down an area of groundbait and chopped bait, which are packed into the feeder for every cast.

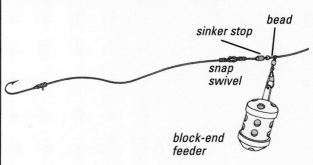

bead
sinker stop
snap swivel
block-end feeder

The block-end feeder is filled with maggots which escape gradually into the water.

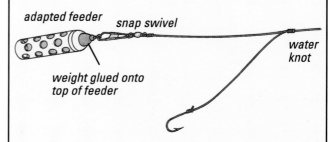

adapted feeder *snap swivel*
water knot
weight glued onto top of feeder

By gluing a weight directly on the end of a feeder, you'll be able to cast your rig farther from shore.

In some parts of the world, fishing with sinkers is called legering. Anglers in these places use sensitive bite detectors called swingtips and quivertips. Swingtips screw into the end of special leger rods, and quivertips are pushed into the end.

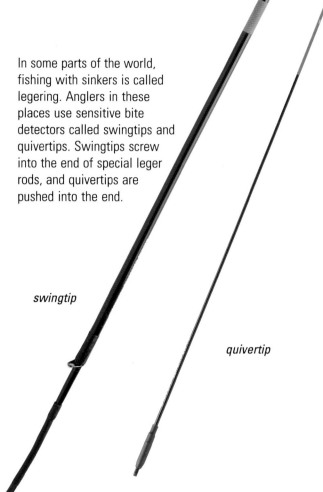

swingtip

quivertip

THE QUIVERTIP

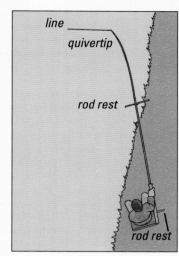

line

quivertip

rod rest

rod rest

The quivertip is a popular form of bite detection. The tackle is cast out and allowed to settle on the bottom. With the rod propped securely on rests, the line is tightened until the quivertip is slightly flexed.

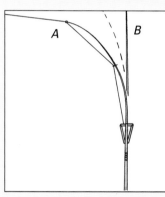

A

B

If the tip bends toward A, the fish has taken the bait and is moving away from the angler. Movement B shows the fish is moving toward the angler. He or she should immediately set the hook.

BUTTS AND BOBBINS

Butt and bobbin indicators are two other bite indicators. You can make a simple bobbin by clipping the cap from a detergent bottle on the line. Set the hook when A or B occurs.

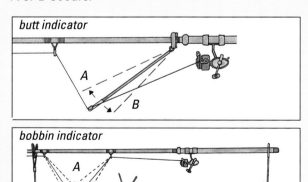

butt indicator

A

B

bobbin indicator

A

B

THE SWINGTIP

The swingtip is another sensitive bite detector – but it can only be used when the water is still.

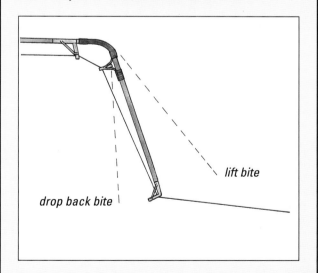

lift bite

drop back bite

POLE FISHING

Pole fishing is a European technique used most widely in France, Italy, and Britain. A pole enables the angler to present bait more delicately and accurately than with a rod and reel. This is a real advantage when trying to catch shy-biting fish.

WHAT IS A POLE?

A pole is simply lots of rodlike sections that can be joined to give the angler a very long reach – some poles are an amazing 33 ft long! Once a fish is hooked, it is brought in by disconnecting the sections. Although the method may at first seem difficult, it is a very quick way of bringing in small fish.

This speed can be invaluable during competitions, when the winner is the angler who catches the greatest weight of fish in the time allowed.

A pole is made up of sections. The most comfortable way to hold it while waiting for a bite is to rest it on your knee.

Pole floats are very light and delicate. They are attached to the line through an eye on the body of the float, and also by a sleeve pushed onto the float's stem. An extra sleeve might be needed for neat presentation of a large-bodied float.

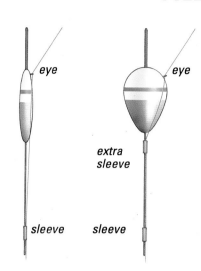

There are three basic shapes of pole float: slim, body down, and body up. Some have wire stems which provide greater stability for fishing in moving water.

slim

body down

body up

FLICK TIP

There's no reel with a pole – instead, the line is connected directly to the tip by one of two methods. The simplest, called a flick tip, is a fine length of solid carbon or fiberglass which is connected to the top joint. A small loop at the end provides a connecting point for the line. A flick tip gives a lightning-fast strike, needed for the tentative or choosy bites of small fish.

POLE ELASTIC

The second method is designed for larger fish. It consists of a length of pole elastic threaded through the top two sections of pole. This acts as a shock absorber when a fish is hooked, lessening the force which would otherwise be borne by the main line or leader.

Pole elastic is color coded. The breaking strain guide below shows the delicacy of the tackle used by pole anglers.

Color	Breaking strain	Leader
White	12 oz/340 g	5-10 oz/140-280 g
Red	1 lb/0.45 kg	10-14 oz/280-400 g
Green	1.25 lb/0.56 kg	12 oz-1.1 lb/340-500 g
Blue	2.25 lb/1 kg	1.1-1.7 lb/0.5-0.8 kg
Black	3 lb/1.4 kg	1.7-2.6 lb/0.8-1.2 kg
Yellow	4 lb/1.8 kg	2.6-3.2 lb/1.2-1.6 kg

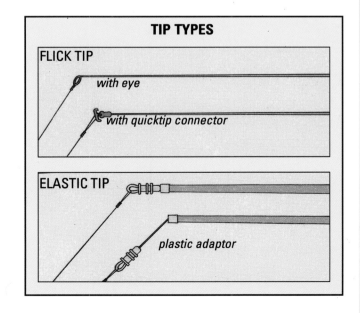

TIP TYPES

FLICK TIP

with eye

with quicktip connector

ELASTIC TIP

plastic adaptor

SINKERS

Where any bulk weight is needed, usually with body-down or body-up floats, sinkers called Olivettes are usually used. Smaller weights, called "styls," are sometimes added beneath the Olivette.

THE CORRECT WEIGHT

You can buy pole rigs already assembled, with the correct weight attached to the line. If you assemble your own rigs, it is best to add the heavier weights first. Fine adjustments to the float's setting can then be made by adding styl weights or shot.

Olivette weights are simply threaded on the line and can be held in place with a tiny shot. Styl weights clamp over the line and should be fixed into place with special pincers.

styl pincers

Olivette

styl weights

POLE RIGS

Rigs for pole fishing consist of a length of main line, a leader, weights, and a float. A 12 oz bs (breaking strain) leader of about 18 in, double looped to a main line of 1-1.5 lb, will be enough for most smaller fish. Where larger fish are expected, in weedy spots, 1.7 lb connected to 2.6 lb would be more appropriate. Have a selection of size 18 to 24 hooks to use with baits such as bread punch and maggots.

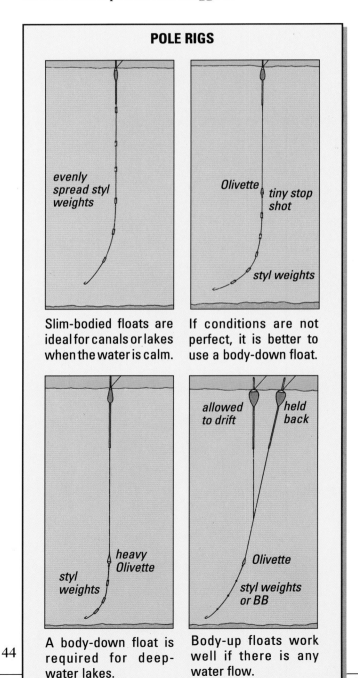

POLE RIGS

evenly spread styl weights

Slim-bodied floats are ideal for canals or lakes when the water is calm.

Olivette | *tiny stop shot* | *styl weights*

If conditions are not perfect, it is better to use a body-down float.

styl weights | *heavy Olivette*

A body-down float is required for deep-water lakes.

allowed to drift | *held back* | *Olivette* | *styl weights or BB*

Body-up floats work well if there is any water flow.

CASTING

Casting, or "putting in" a pole, can be done in two ways. When a short length of pole is being used, the tackle can be swung out under the pole. If there is a stiff breeze, an overhead cast may be necessary.

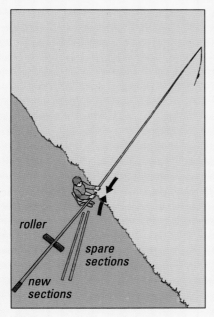

feed area

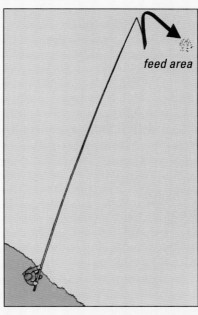

feed area

With a long pole, add new sections to the butt end. A pole roller will allow you to attach and remove several sections at once.

Carefully push out the pole until you've added enough sections to reach the feed area.

Gently lower the line, float, and bait into the feed area.

It's best to assemble pole rigs at home, because it's a fairly complicated job. Assembled rigs should be wound onto a winder and held in position with a nylon clip or a pole-rig anchor, where they will stay neat and untangled.

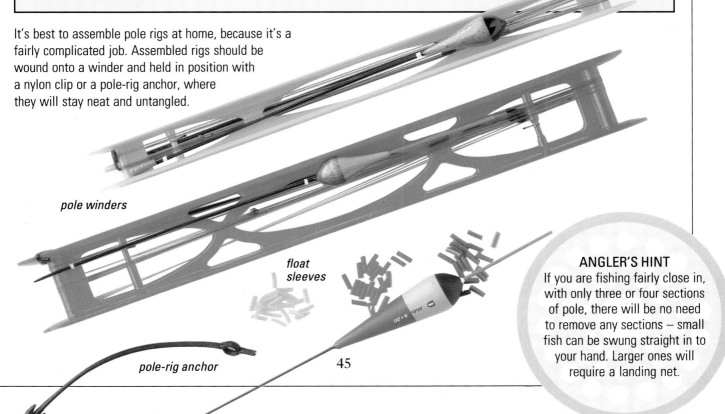

pole winders

float sleeves

pole-rig anchor

ANGLER'S HINT
If you are fishing fairly close in, with only three or four sections of pole, there will be no need to remove any sections — small fish can be swung straight in to your hand. Larger ones will require a landing net.

FISHING FOR PREDATORS

Predatory fish, such as pike, perch, and large trout, are the tigers of the river. They have needle-sharp teeth and fight ferociously, so you'll have a *real* battle on your hands when you hook one of these voracious hunters. Get your catch close to the bank, and it'll fight even harder!

TACKLE

Heavier tackle is needed to cope with these fierce, heavy fish and the larger baits required. Your spinning reel should have a deep spool loaded with 200 yd of 10- to 12-lb line.

You may want to use a wire leader so your prey doesn't bite through the line. You will also need a large landing net.

FISHING A BAIT

Freelining is the simplest method of bait fishing for large predators. It uses only a bait mounted on a single hook. Treble hooks, which are three single hooks soldered together, are also often used. After you have cast out, leave the bale arm open and wait for the bait to settle on the bottom. You will know this has happened when the line goes slack.

If you wish, you may place the rod on a couple of rests. The front rest can even be an electronic bite indicator, a piece of European equipment, available in some U.S. speciality stores, that will emit a bleeping noise when a fish takes the bait! The set-up (shown in the diagram above) will be more sensitive if a simple bobbin or "monkey climb" indicator is used, too. The "monkey climb" bobbin moves up and down a pole and so is less affected by wind. Leave the bale arm open so that when a fish takes the bait there will be no resistance to cause it to drop the bait.

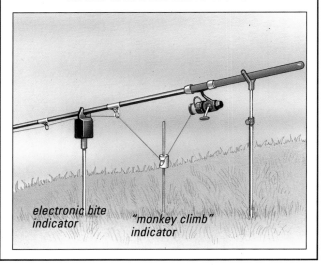

EUROPEAN BITE INDICATORS

electronic bite indicator

"monkey climb" indicator

Predatory fish, especially pike and large perch, do not hunt in open water. Instead, they lie in wait in reeds and other underwater growth, ready to ambush any prey that swims within striking distance. Depressions in the lake or river bed also make ideal ambush points.

bay

46

submerged willows

RIGS FOR LARGE BAITS

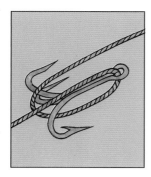

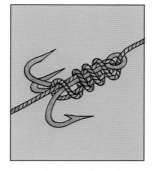

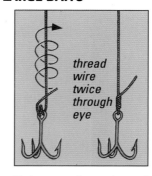

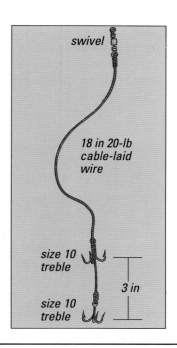

To make a rig for fishing medium to large baits, thread the end of a 18 in length of cable-laid wire through the eye of a size 10 treble hook and push the hook along the wire about 4 in.

Wrap the wire four times around the shank and back through the eye. Put corks or pieces of plastic foam over the hook points so you don't injure yourself while you add a second hook.

Take another size 10 treble hook and fasten it to the end. Trim off any extra wire with wire cutters. Fasten a swivel to the other end of the wire, using the same method of attachment as for the bottom hook.

thread wire twice through eye

swivel

18 in 20-lb cable-laid wire

size 10 treble

size 10 treble

3 in

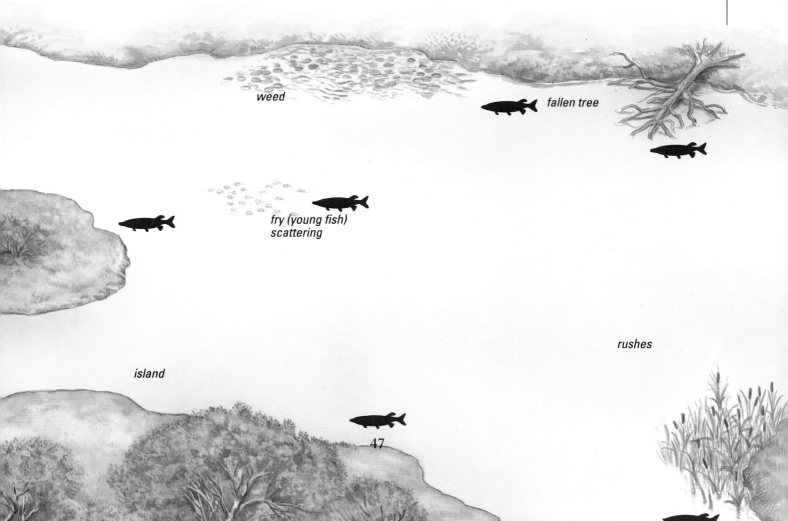

weed

fallen tree

fry (young fish) scattering

island

rushes

FISH BAITS

Predatory fish feed mainly on other fish, so a dead fish bait can be very effective. You can buy it at almost any bait and tackle shop. Herrings, mackerel, and mullet are all good baits.

Alternatively, devote a fishing session to catching bait, then keep it in a freezer until you need it. Large whole baits are ideal for pike and bass; smaller ones are better for perch and sunfish. Baits should be killed humanely as soon as they are caught.

DEADBAIT FLOAT RIGS

The deadbait float shown on the next page is a relatively elaborate rig, designed for fishing a lake bed covered with weed. The bait is suspended above the bottom and so is more easily seen by a predator. This method is particularly suitable for catching fish that are at home in murky conditions.

WOBBLED BAITS

If you prefer to fish more actively, cast and then retrieve the bait using the reel. The bait will wobble in the water, like a swimming fish, and will attract predators. This method is best suited to a lake which has lots of shallow bays and inlets, or a river. Vary the speed of retrieve and also the depths at which you fish the bait.

MOUNTING DEADBAITS

MEDIUM TO LARGE BAIT

tie with line to prevent bait flying off during cast

HALF-FISH BAIT

SMALL BAIT

FLOAT-RIG SET-UP

WOBBLED BAIT SET-UP

A magnificent river pike – a fearsome predator.

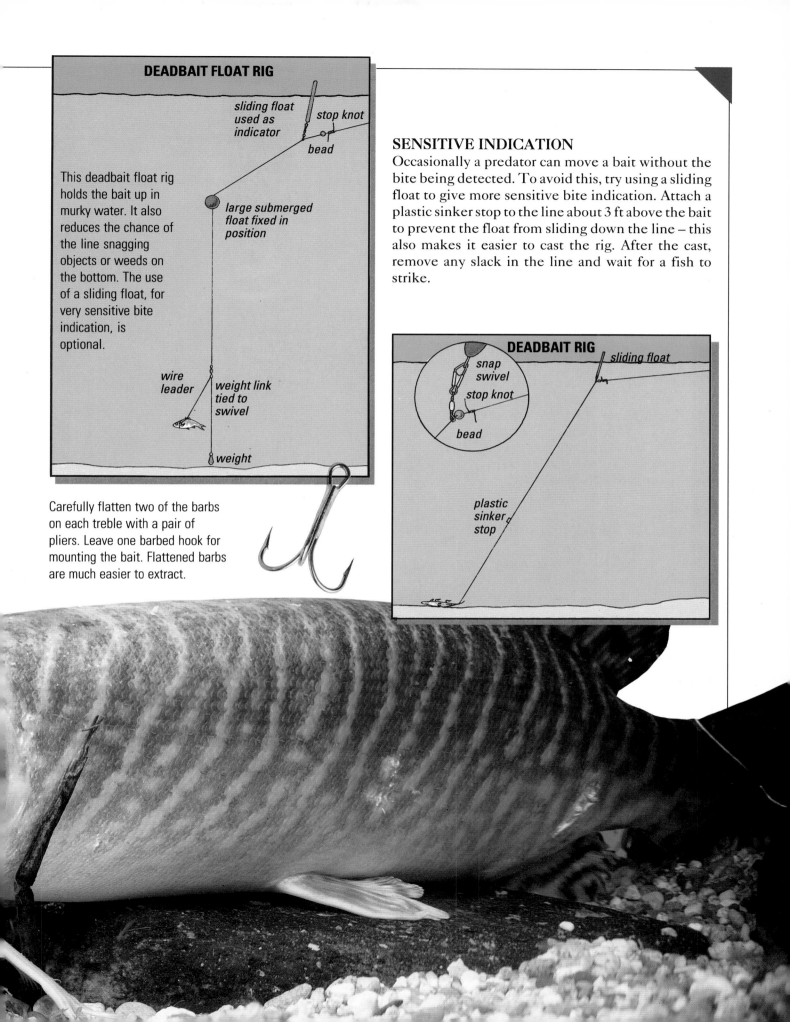

DEADBAIT FLOAT RIG

sliding float used as indicator

stop knot

bead

This deadbait float rig holds the bait up in murky water. It also reduces the chance of the line snagging objects or weeds on the bottom. The use of a sliding float, for very sensitive bite indication, is optional.

large submerged float fixed in position

wire leader

weight link tied to swivel

weight

Carefully flatten two of the barbs on each treble with a pair of pliers. Leave one barbed hook for mounting the bait. Flattened barbs are much easier to extract.

SENSITIVE INDICATION

Occasionally a predator can move a bait without the bite being detected. To avoid this, try using a sliding float to give more sensitive bite indication. Attach a plastic sinker stop to the line about 3 ft above the bait to prevent the float from sliding down the line – this also makes it easier to cast the rig. After the cast, remove any slack in the line and wait for a fish to strike.

DEADBAIT RIG

sliding float

snap swivel

stop knot

bead

plastic sinker stop

SPINNERS, SPOONS, AND PLUGS

Perch, pike, trout, and bass all respond to artificial baits, called lures. If you do not want to wait for a predator to pick up your static deadbait, this active method is worth trying.

ON THE MOVE
Mobility is the key with lure fishing. All you really need is your rod, a landing net, and a bag. Carry an assortment of lures (in a lure box, so you don't hook yourself), a soft gardening glove and a disgorger for removing hooks, an assortment of swivels, and a few anti-kink vanes or weights. Also carry a pair of pliers for making repairs to your tackle.

RODS AND REELS
Rods for lure fishing (called spinning rods) have large-diameter line guides to give better casting. Choose a rod with hard-wearing guides that can withstand the constant rubbing of the line. If the rod feels right – be it 7 ft, 8 ft, or 9 ft – that's the one for you.

A spinning reel with 6-lb line can be used with small lures where the fish aren't very big, but you'll need 10- or 12-lb line where larger predators lurk.

SWIVEL AND TWIST
Many wire leaders have a swivel on one end and a snap swivel on the other. The snap swivel is the connecting point for the lure, allowing it to be changed in seconds.

Line twist can be a problem, especially with a rotating lure. You can overcome it by attaching an anti-kink vane to the line just above the top swivel. The vane acts like a keel when the lure is retrieved, cutting straight through the water and forcing the swivel to function properly as the lure turns.

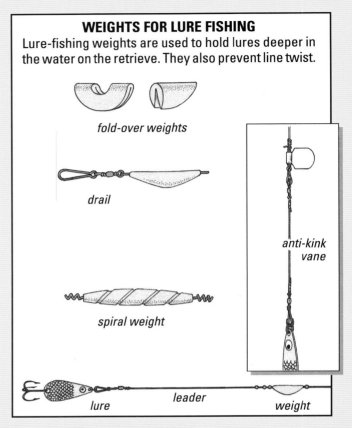

WEIGHTS FOR LURE FISHING
Lure-fishing weights are used to hold lures deeper in the water on the retrieve. They also prevent line twist.

fold-over weights

drail

spiral weight

anti-kink vane

lure   leader   weight

Lures mimic real fish. Spinners whirl as they are dragged through the water, while spoons wriggle and wobble like a wounded fish. Plugs vary in their action. Some skitter along the surface when retrieved, others float on the surface when stationary and dive when retrieved.

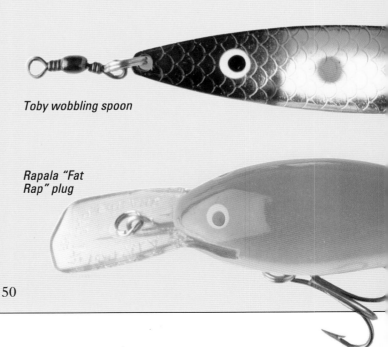

Toby wobbling spoon

Rapala "Fat Rap" plug

very steep dive   *shallow dive*   *on or near surface*

Some plugs have an adjustable diving vane, on the nose, to set the diving motion.

ABU Droppen spinner

Rapala jointed plug

A short spinning rod is easier to handle in a boat. Many good river pike will be found almost under the bank, out of the main current. Cast downstream, then work the lure back toward you.

51

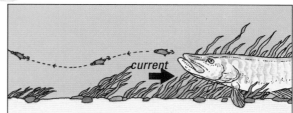
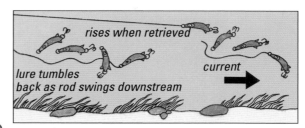

SURF CASTING

What's the attraction of surf casting? There's fabulous scenery, you may not need a license, and the fish taste great! However, success in surf casting, whether from the shore or a boat, depends a lot on a knowledge of the tide. Buy a tide table so you will know when the water is high – generally the best time for fishing. When the water is low, it is a good time for gathering bait.

STAY WARM AND DRY
Always carry extra clothing and a hat in case you feel your body temperature dropping. Rubber boots are ideal for beach fishing, but boat shoes are better suited to slippery boat decks. Neoprene mittens will keep your hands warm – and a quick wring when they become wet will easily dry them.

THE SURF CASTING ROD
For fishing from a beach you will need a surf rod, a powerful rod capable of casting long distances. Choose one as large as you can comfortably hold. Make sure it's designed for use with a spinning reel and has a large line guide on the bottom section.

REEL AND LINE
A spinning reel used for surf casting will produce long, trouble-free casts. Buy a carbon model with stainless steel bearings, to resist saltwater corrosion; it should accomodate at least 200 yd of 15-lb line.

A 15-lb line is adequate for open, sandy beaches, but in rocky areas something stronger is needed. In any case, tie 10 yd of heavier line to the front end of the main line as a safety precaution. This "shock leader" will prevent the weight from snapping off during the cast. Increase the shock leader's strength for heavier casting weights, e.g., 3-oz weight – 30-lb leader; 4-oz weight – 40-lb; 5-oz weight – 50-lb, and so on.

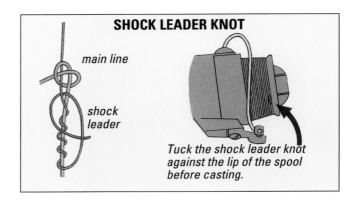

SHOCK LEADER KNOT

main line

shock leader

Tuck the shock leader knot against the lip of the spool before casting.

Although you will be close to the water's edge when fishing from a beach, it is best to keep the bulk of your equipment some distance back from the rising tide, out of harm's way.

ANGLER'S HINT
Always go fishing with an adult. Make sure a rising tide won't cut off your fishing position, and never fish from rocks when the sea is very rough.

LARGE HOOKS

Large hooks come in a variety of designs. Finer hooks like the Aberdeen are used for flatfish such as flounders and fluke; heavier ones like the O'Shaughnessy are required for powerful fish such as cod or pollack.

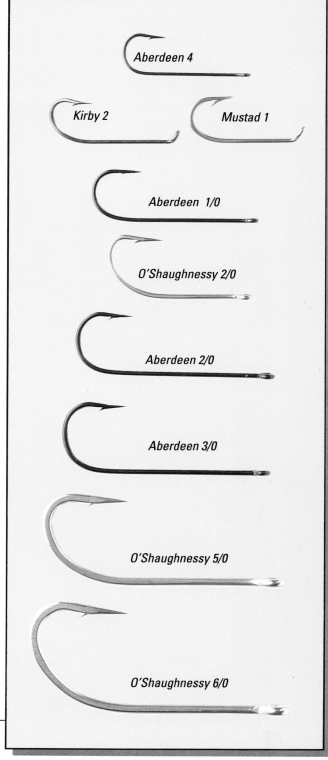

Aberdeen 4

Kirby 2

Mustad 1

Aberdeen 1/0

O'Shaughnessy 2/0

Aberdeen 2/0

Aberdeen 3/0

O'Shaughnessy 5/0

O'Shaughnessy 6/0

AN OFF-THE-GROUND CAST

There are several ways of casting from the shore, some of them quite complicated and requiring special rods. This off-the-ground cast is suitable for a standard surf rod. Always make sure that no-one is standing close to you.

direction of cast

line trapped

bale arm open

Stand almost side on to the direction of the cast. Turn your body to hold the rod behind you, keeping your weight on your back foot. Rest the bait on the ground.

Pull the rod forward across your chest, turning forward as you do. You should begin to transfer your weight toward your front foot.

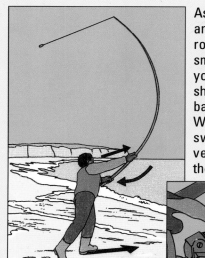

As your upper hand and arm push the rod strongly and smoothly forward, your lower hand should pull the butt back into the body. When the rod is swung past the vertical, release the line.

MORE AT THE SEASHORE

There are not many places along the shore that are without fish. Beaches, rocks, harbor walls, jetties, and piers are all worth exploring with a rod and line. However, the fish are not evenly distributed along the coast, and what may be a good spot one day may yield very little the next. Plan your fishing trip carefully, taking into account the tides and weather, to get the most from your visit to the shore.

FINDING THE FISH

Fish will be found where there's food. A gently sloping beach will provide rich pickings for bass just after a storm, whereas in calm weather the bass might be feeding elsewhere, such as among rocks. Fishing from a pier or jetty might produce nothing on a low tide but could provide non-stop action when the water is high.

Spring through fall is generally the best time of year to cast a bait from the shore. This is when many species move close to the shoreline. They also swim up estuaries (river mouths) and creeks in search of food. Good shore fishing can also be had in the winter in the southern United States.

This huge conger eel was caught near a harbor wall, where there are many feeding opportunities for fish. When you arrive at a beach, just prior to the tide coming in, position your base so you will be casting into a feature such as a gully between fingers of rock. When it is covered by the rising tide, this bit of the sea bed will trap food and become a restaurant for fish.

Use a rod rest when bites are scarce, and to hold your rod and reel clear of sand when you change bait or tackle. You can make your own rest from a piece of PVC piping, or buy one from a speciality store. A monopod can be used on firm, sandy beaches, while the bulkier tripod is designed for rocks and harbor walls.

ANGLER'S HINT
Try threading a couple of colored plastic beads on the line, just above the hook, as an added attraction for fish — it really works!

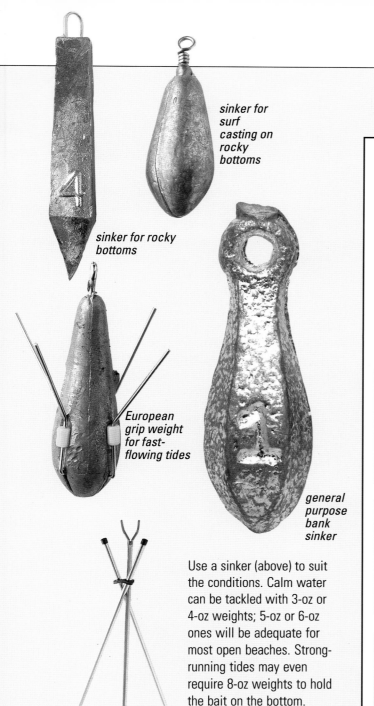

sinker for surf casting on rocky bottoms

sinker for rocky bottoms

European grip weight for fast-flowing tides

general purpose bank sinker

Use a sinker (above) to suit the conditions. Calm water can be tackled with 3-oz or 4-oz weights; 5-oz or 6-oz ones will be adequate for most open beaches. Strong-running tides may even require 8-oz weights to hold the bait on the bottom.

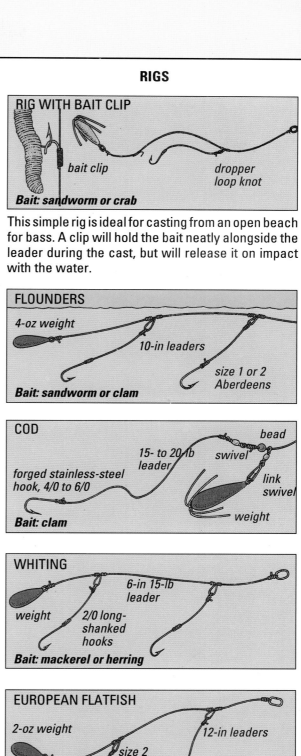

RIGS

RIG WITH BAIT CLIP

bait clip

dropper loop knot

Bait: sandworm or crab

This simple rig is ideal for casting from an open beach for bass. A clip will hold the bait neatly alongside the leader during the cast, but will release it on impact with the water.

FLOUNDERS

4-oz weight

10-in leaders

size 1 or 2 Aberdeens

Bait: sandworm or clam

COD

bead

15- to 20-lb leader

swivel

forged stainless-steel hook, 4/0 to 6/0

link swivel

weight

Bait: clam

WHITING

6-in 15-lb leader

weight

2/0 long-shanked hooks

Bait: mackerel or herring

EUROPEAN FLATFISH

2-oz weight

12-in leaders

size 2 Aberdeen hooks

Bait: sandworm or piece of crab

FISHING FROM ROCKS

It is not always necessary to hurl a bait far out to sea in order to catch a decent-size fish. During warm weather you might look down from a rocky perch or jetty and see large fish swimming below. They could be mullet, browsing among the weed, or bass looking for prawns. Even a school of mackerel could suddenly appear right beneath your feet as they herd frantic sand eels ahead of them.

HARBORS

Interesting fishing can often be had in the shelter of harbors, especially when fishing boats are unloading their catch – again, you will often find fish directly beneath your rod. The two hours each side of high tide will often provide the most action.

A surf-casting rod is too cumbersome for harbor fishing. Use something with a more sensitive tip, such as a spinning rod. Line can also be lighter – 8 lb to 10 lb should be adequate.

ESTUARIES

Farther up the estuary, flounders can provide non-stop action at high tide as they move out of the main river channel and over the submerged flats in search of food. Pieces of sand worm are the ideal bait for these flatfish – and, unfortunately, for most crabs, too.

Once again, long casts are seldom needed. A 10-lb line, used with a light surf caster or a spinning rod, will be strong enough.

You don't have to go onto a beach or rocks to find exciting fishing. Jetties and harbor walls are ideal sites for anglers with limited mobility.

Have a friend help you with a landing net to land large fish from a steeply sloping beach or other difficult situation. Use a long-handled net when fishing from rocks – it's too dangerous to lean over the water and grab a fish by hand.

Where you are some distance above the water, have a drop net ready to hoist up fish of 1 lb or more.

SNAGS

Snagging the bottom is a problem when fishing among rocks, so attach the weight to the main line with a leader of lower breaking-strain line. If your weight becomes snagged, point the rod straight at the snag and pull steadily to break the weaker line. Your rig will be intact, minus only the weight.

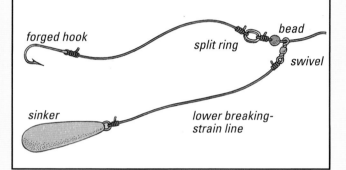

FLOAT FISHING

This is very effective in rocky areas. Predators such as bluefish and bass are attracted to the natural movement of the bait as it rises and falls with the sea. Also, there's less chance of snags if the float is holding the bait clear of underwater obstructions.

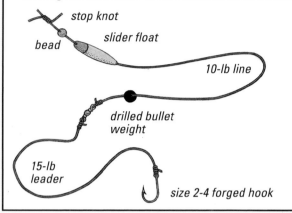

Rocks provide a good vantage point for the angler. The best time is summer, when large bass can often be found close in, especially when the high tide occurs at dawn or dusk.

Always wear protective footgear when wading in the water! Hidden hazards waiting to be stepped on at the shore include stingrays (which can inflict a painful wound with their whiplike tails), crabs, fish hooks, and garbage. The spines of the European weaver fish (below), which lies half buried in the sand in shallow water, can be painful if stepped on.

BOAT FISHING

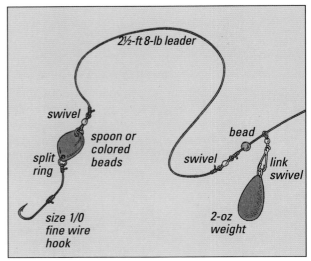

FISHING FOR FLOUNDERS

2½-ft 8-lb leader

swivel

split ring

spoon or colored beads

size 1/0 fine wire hook

bead

swivel

link swivel

2-oz weight

When fishing for flounders, tackle needs to be light – try using a spinning rod and reel loaded with 8- to 10-lb line.

Flounders respond well to a couple of colored beads, just above the bait. These extra attractors move enticingly in the tide's flow.

If you have relatives or friends with boats, you're in luck – good boat fishing can be had inshore, in sheltered estuaries and bays, as well as offshore, on the open sea. *Always* go with an adult companion who has experience with boats and knows the area.

BOAT SENSE
Only go out in a properly equipped boat, and never go out in bad weather. Wear a life jacket at all times and, once afloat, *never* stand up in a small boat – everything can be done from a sitting position.

Always have a landing net on board when you are fishing from a boat. It is easy enough to swing small fish onboard, but don't risk lifting larger ones out with the rod. Also, take a cushion, because some boat seats are very uncomfortable.

FINDING THE FISH
As the tide rises in the estuary, fish will move in from the open sea. Depending on your location, bass, surf perch, and even mackerel can be encountered during the summer months. Bass are partial to sand worms and are sometimes caught while fishing for flounder.

Mackerel will be visible as they chase schools of small fry, causing the water surface to boil with activity. A lure such as a Toby (see pages 50-51) cast across the front of the school will almost certainly produce a take. If you don't have a spare spinning rod already assembled, use a snap swivel to change, in seconds, to a shiny lure.

If you see a school of mackerel moving up an estuary, cast and retrieve a lure across the school.

cast here

58

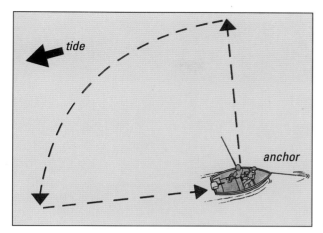

The tackle can be cast across the tide and allowed to swing around in an arc, then retrieved very slowly.

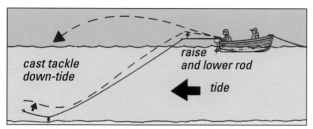

You can also cast directly down-tide. Raise and lower the tackle at intervals.

RED DRUM

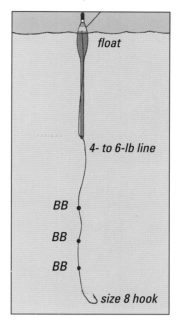

Small red drums will feed in rivers and estuaries. If the fish are not biting, try a light float rig with a natural bait, such as shrimp, to tempt this stubborn fighter.

float

4- to 6-lb line

BB

BB

BB

size 8 hook

tide

A bait trail can be used to attract fish to your boat. Hang a cloth sack filled with chum, a mixture of chopped fish or mollusks, over the stern of the boat.

tidal flow

retrieve

direction of school

OFFSHORE BOAT FISHING RIGS

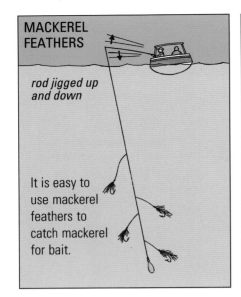

MACKEREL FEATHERS

rod jigged up and down

It is easy to use mackerel feathers to catch mackerel for bait.

If tackle tangles are a problem, use a three-way swivel or a plastic boom to hold the leader away from the main line. Open the bale arm and let the weight sink to the bottom. Wind in line so the weight is just clear of the bottom.

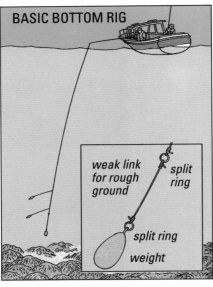

BASIC BOTTOM RIG

weak link for rough ground

split ring

split ring

weight

Set the hook when a fish takes the bait. With the redgill lure, retrieve the rig steadily. Predatory fish such as cod or pollack will hook themselves as they snatch the lure.

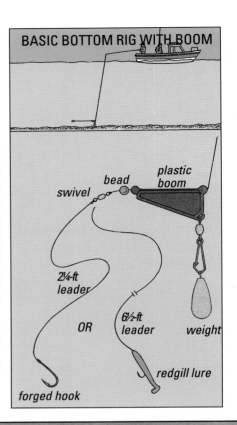

BASIC BOTTOM RIG WITH BOOM

swivel

bead

plastic boom

2¼-ft leader

OR

6½-ft leader

weight

redgill lure

forged hook

OFFSHORE BOAT FISHING

Licensed charter boats take anglers to offshore sites to fish for a wide variety of species. What you catch will be determined by the season and your location. Rough ground is the favorite haunt of dogfish. Banks of gravel support a large variety of fish such as cod, turbot, ling, and halibut. Banks of mud are feeding grounds for whiting, and reefs can be relied upon to produce pollack, whiting, and grouper.

On the way out you may slow down to catch mackerel for bait. This can be done using lures called mackerel feathers. Sometimes you'll catch a mackerel on every feather, and plenty of bait can be caught in a very short time.

Saltwater boat reels give a greater feeling of being in contact with the fish. However, line can come off the reel's drum too fast during casting, creating horrible tangles. Lots of practice and experience is needed before one can be used confidently.

BOAT FISHING

EQUIPMENT

When boat fishing offshore, tackle needs vary greatly depending on the kind of fish you are trying to catch. For a beginner, a 20- to 30-lb-class 7-ft rod, coupled with a good quality saltwater boat reel (loaded with 20- to 30-lb test line), is a good, all-purpose combo.

Be careful when setting the reel's drag because a large fish could easily be lost if the drag is set too tight. On the other hand, setting a reel's drag too loose could prevent you from successfully setting the hook. Always set the drag correctly to yield line. Use the rod to take the strain as you use a slow up-and-down pumping action, reeling in slack line as the rod is lowered.

Sandeel lures (below) and rubber squid (right) can be used to attract predators such as cod or ling.

sandeels

rubber squid

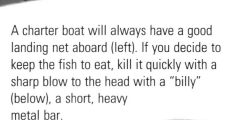

A charter boat will always have a good landing net aboard (left). If you decide to keep the fish to eat, kill it quickly with a sharp blow to the head with a "billy" (below), a short, heavy metal bar.

billy

ANGLER'S HINT
Bring along a pair of polarized sunglasses when you go fishing. They will not only make you more comfortable on a bright day, but will help you see under the water's surface.

SEA-FISHING BAITS

Although you can buy sea-fishing baits from tackle shops, it is cheaper – and more fun – to collect them yourself. Provided it is stored properly, the bait will stay alive and healthy for a couple of days. Estuaries are often good bait hunting areas but they are dangerous if you don't leave well before the tide begins to rise. It is easier and more sensible to search for bait along the shore. For example, open sandy beaches, close to the low water mark, provide good areas for lugworm. Only go bait hunting with an adult who knows the area well.

CRAB

Shore crabs that are casting, or losing, their old shell make an excellent bait for bass, flounders, dabs, and cod. They can be found beneath weed-covered rock. Store them in a bucket with wet seaweed and cover the top with a towel soaked in sea water.

LUGWORM

These worms create their familiar casts near the low water mark on sand or mud beaches. Dig for them between the cast and the hole. Lugworms are a good bait for cod, whiting, and bass. They are best used on the day you dig them, but will survive for a few days wrapped in newspaper.

CLAMWORM

Clamworms live in estuaries and harbors. Used whole, they make good bait for striped bass and other game fish. When cut into sections they are excellent for flounder. A clamworm's jaws can inflict a painful bite, so grip the worm firmly right behind its head. Store clamworms in damp seaweed in a cool place.

crab (with shell)

crab (with shell discarded)

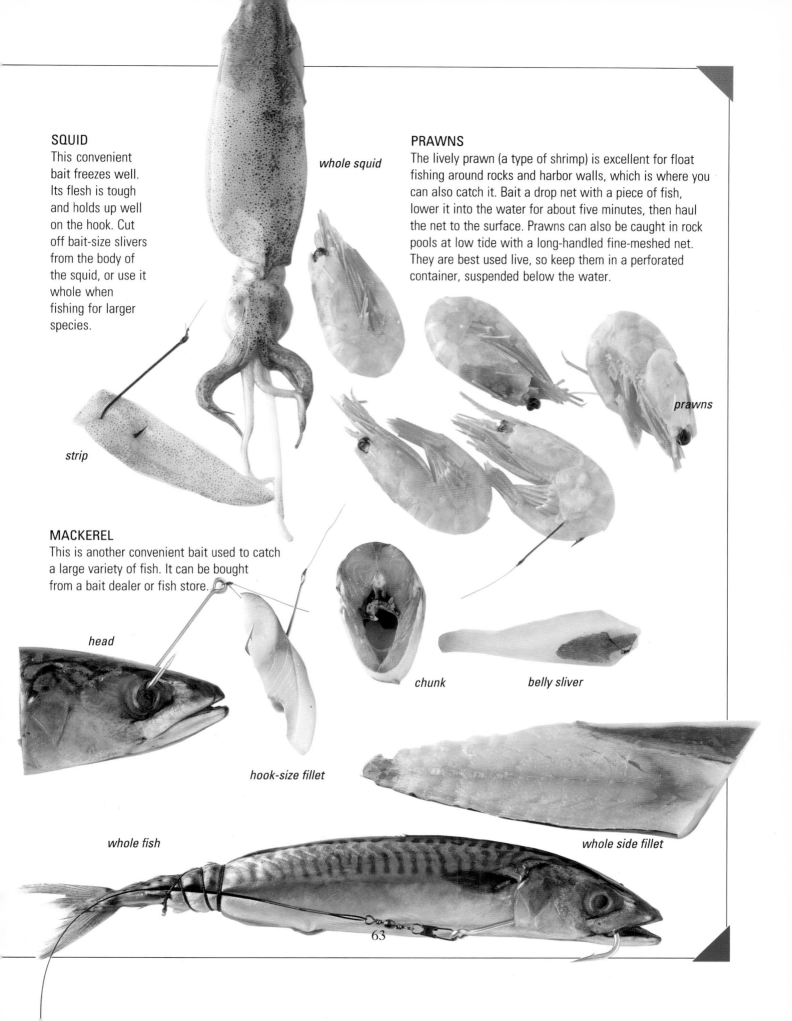

SQUID

This convenient bait freezes well. Its flesh is tough and holds up well on the hook. Cut off bait-size slivers from the body of the squid, or use it whole when fishing for larger species.

whole squid

strip

PRAWNS

The lively prawn (a type of shrimp) is excellent for float fishing around rocks and harbor walls, which is where you can also catch it. Bait a drop net with a piece of fish, lower it into the water for about five minutes, then haul the net to the surface. Prawns can also be caught in rock pools at low tide with a long-handled fine-meshed net. They are best used live, so keep them in a perforated container, suspended below the water.

prawns

MACKEREL

This is another convenient bait used to catch a large variety of fish. It can be bought from a bait dealer or fish store.

head

chunk

belly sliver

hook-size fillet

whole side fillet

whole fish

63

FLY FISHING

Fly fishing is considered the most sporting method of angling. It uses an artificial "fly" to imitate the insects or small fish that are the food of game fish such as trout. Fly fishing is easier than is commonly thought – it is only the method of casting that you might find difficult. You can teach yourself to cast, or learn from an experienced fly angler. Alternatively, pay for lessons with a professional instructor, who will provide tackle for the lessons.

The secret to successful fly fishing is presentation of the fly. Don't be distracted from learning good technique by the many flashy fly designs available.

ROD
Begin with a fly rod of about 8½ ft, suitable for casting a No. 6 line. Look at the rod, just in front of the handle, for a number or numbers. These indicate what line will perform most efficiently with the rod. A rod marked 5, 6, or 7 will provide the right balance for the beginner.

REEL
A fly reel should be able to hold a 30-yd fly line attached to backing line. Backing line is wound onto the reel first to provide a good bed for the main fly line, and for when a running fish strips all the fly line from the reel. Choose a reel with a standard size of spool, rather than a wide spool made to take heavier lines, e.g., No. 7 up, and extra backing line.

LINE
There are two main types of fly line, called double taper (DT) and weight forward (WF). There are also lines that float and lines that sink, some very slowly and others quickly. A "double-taper No. 6 floater" is good to start with: it falls lightly on the water and is also easy to lift off the surface for your next cast. The specification on the pack should read DT6F (double-taper – 6 – floater).

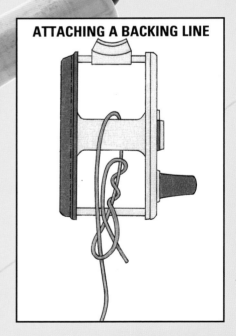

ATTACHING A BACKING LINE

Backing line comes on 165-ft or 250-ft spools and is tied to the reel as shown above. A braided leader butt (see page 66) makes a good connector between the backing and the line.

A moment of great excitement – hooking a fine trout. Now it has to be landed!

A correctly loaded reel. The line should lie clear of the reel's horizontal casing supports.

ANATOMY OF AN ARTIFICIAL FLY

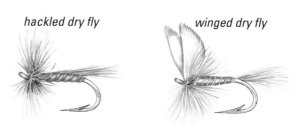

ARTIFICIAL FLIES

hackled dry fly   *winged dry fly*

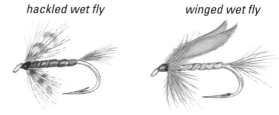

Dry flies imitate insects that are floating on the surface. They are made buoyant by applying a spray known as "floatant."

hackled wet fly   *winged wet fly*

Wet flies are fished below the surface. They imitate drowned insects or, in the case of the more flashy patterns, small fish.

Nymphs are fished at various depths beneath the surface and imitate the stage before the aquatic insect emerges as an adult.

Lures and streamer flies are meant to give the impression of small fish. Many patterns look nothing like fish but are nevertheless effective.

LEADERS

A leader is a link between the fly and the fly line. Level line can work quite well, but straighter, cleaner casts are produced with a tapered leader. The butt, or thicker end, is connected to the line and the tippet, the finer end, is tied to the fly. The most advanced leaders are made from braided nylon. These braided leaders are fairly expensive but give good casts. A nylon monofilament tippet will still have to be connected to the thin end of the braid, and changed from time to time, but the main part of the leader will last indefinitely.

Lengths cut from spools of 6-lb, 4-lb, and 3-lb fly leader monofilament line (below) can be tied together using the water knot to make a tapered leader. Cut a single length of line to make a tippet for a braided leader.

main line

braided leader

monofilament tippet

fly

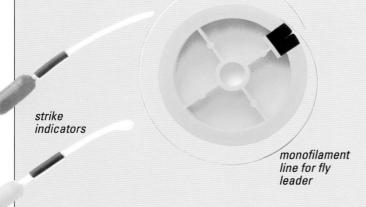

strike indicators

monofilament line for fly leader

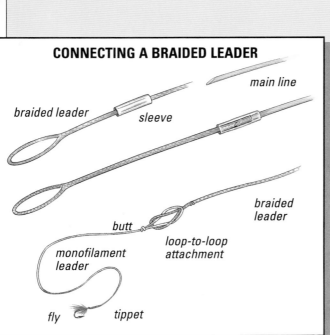

CONNECTING A BRAIDED LEADER

braided leader

sleeve

main line

butt

loop-to-loop attachment

braided leader

monofilament leader

fly

tippet

A reel with main line and leaders (above). Strike indicators (above left) are like miniature floats. They are attached to the leader, and signal a take when a nymph is being fished.

66

LEARNING TO CAST

Learning to cast involves lots of practice. The object is to throw a length of line straight out in front of you, onto the water surface. You will not need any water – a large lawn or field will do just as well. There is no need to connect the leader to the line when practicing.

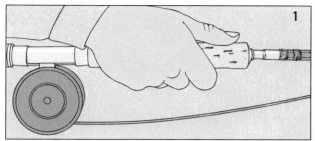

Grip the rod, with the thumb lying along the top of the handle and the reel hanging directly downward.

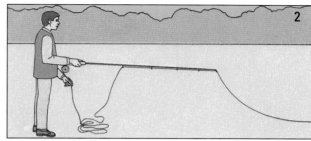

Hold the rod horizontally with about a rod length of line beyond the tip. Pull off some line from the reel.

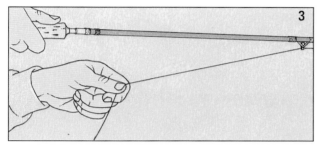

Hold the line with your free hand somewhere between the bottom line guide and the handle.

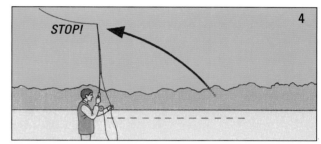

Lift the rod briskly from the horizontal to the vertical position and bring it to an abrupt stop. The line beyond the rod tip will sail back, up and behind you. Do not, on any back cast movement, allow the line to drop.

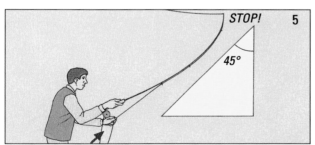

Drive the rod tip forward through 45° and again bring it to an abrupt stop while allowing some of the line, pulled from the reel, to slide from your free hand.

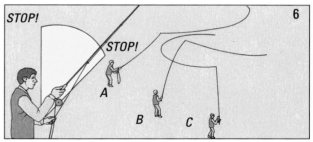

As the airborne line unrolls in front of you (A), grip once again with your free hand and bring the rod briskly back to the vertical position (B), and again bring it to an abrupt stop (C). (As you do this, imagine that you are standing with your back against a high brick wall.)

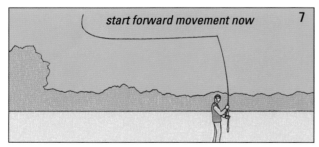

By now you should have extra airborne line, and it will be a help if you watch the line straightening out behind you. Start the forward movement just as the line is straightening out and before it begins to fall behind you.

Now, with enough line in the air, a final cast can be made. As the line unrolls in front of you again, release the grip of your free hand and the line will sail out to fall in a straight line.

FLY FISHING ON STILL WATERS

The many small fisheries that are stocked regularly with rainbow and brown trout provide the ideal place to start fly fishing. Many of them also contain very large trout, so it is a wise precaution to use a tippet of 6 lb bs, going down to 4 lb only if you are presenting a very tiny fly.

TIME FOR THE NYMPH

During the warmer months you will see fish swirling just beneath the surface. It is likely that they are feeding on ascending nymphs. There are many imitation nymphs for situations like this.

Some artificial nymphs are weighted with lead wire and will sink fairly quickly to the bottom. When retrieved, the nymph starts to rise and give a realistic impression of the real creature swimming toward the surface. It is good practice to have a longer than normal leader – 13 ft or so – when fishing a nymph at depth, though it is less easy to control and will take some getting used to. Fish might take nymphs at any depth, so vary the depth of your retrieve until you find where they are feeding.

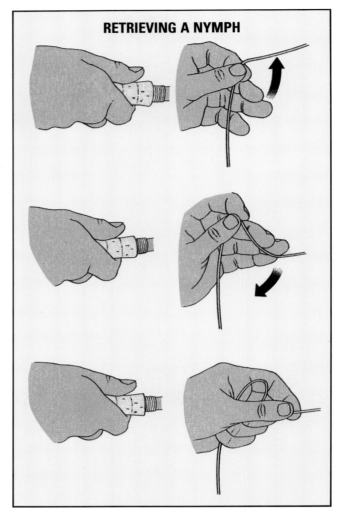

RETRIEVING A NYMPH

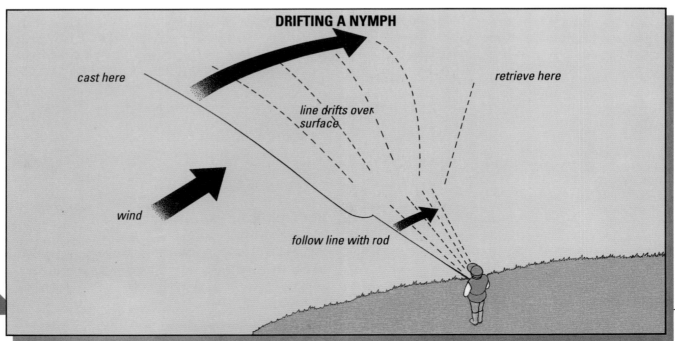

DRIFTING A NYMPH

cast here

retrieve here

line drifts over surface

wind

follow line with rod

Midge pupa, damselfly nymph, and sedge pupa imitations, to name but a few, all work if presented correctly.

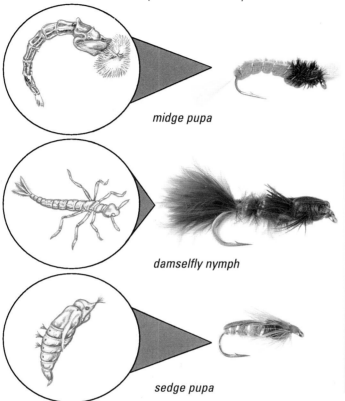

midge pupa

damselfly nymph

sedge pupa

HOW TO FISH THE MIDGE

Stillwater trout feed avidly where there is a concentration of midge pupae. These hang in the tension of the surface layer before turning into adult midges. A fine tippet is a must for fishing a midge. You should also apply floatant to the tippet.

Look for fish rising with the porpoise-like humping movement typical of midge-eating trout. Drop your fly about 10 ft in front of a rising fish. If the fish stays on course, it should see your fly and take it.

trout feeding on midge pupae

cast here

Don't be tempted to lift a fish out like this – the leader is likely to break. Always bring the fish to a net.

The water in many lakes is so crystal clear that the trout will only be deceived by an imitation tied to the finest tippet.

ANGLER'S HINT:
A short length of fluorescent drinking straw attached where the line joins the leader will make an easily visible bite indicator for when a trout takes a nymph.

WHEN TO USE A LURE

If there is no surface activity, usually when the weather is cold or when a bright sun shines high in the sky on a windless day, use a lure to arouse deep-lying, lazy trout. A sinking line is needed to keep the lure at a constant depth during the retrieve.

You will often see some anglers hauling lures back at incredible speeds, but a slow retrieve is often more productive – and cuts down on the number of tiring casts you have to make. Sometimes, as you retrieve, you will feel a fish plucking at the lure. Don't be tempted to jerk or make a half-hearted strike – just keep retrieving. If the trout is interested enough it will take the lure properly and usually hook itself.

Wet flies and streamers can be used when the trout are chasing fish fry. Cast into the disturbance and use an erratic "wounded fish" retrieve. The flies shown below have all been designed to imitate fish fry.

TIME FOR THE DRY FLY

If you see fish splashing on the surface near the shore, they are probably feeding on insects being blown onto the water. Cast a dry fly treated with floatant. Look on the bank upwind of the splashing for the insects you need to imitate.

These are fly patterns, or designs, for deep lure fishing.

Viva

Black Matuka

Orange Marabou

Missionary

Yellow Mohican

Jersey Herd

Sweeney Todd

FLY FISHING ON STILL WATERS

When a trout takes your fly, wait for the line to start moving away before setting the hook. If your fly is ignored, give it a twitch along the surface, because fish often snatch up struggling crane flies and other insects. After catching a fish, always dry off the fly and re-treat it with floatant.

Many black imitations will work when trying to imitate some types of flies – size being more important than accurate imitation. Use a dry fly with a fat body if beetles or ants are around. Crane flies have a unique shape, so keep a couple of "daddy-long-legs" imitations in your fly box, too.

hawthorn fly　　　　*crane fly*

FISHING FROM A BOAT

It is great fun fishing from a boat, but only go out with an adult who is experienced in using one. This is a custom-built fly-fishing boat that is very stable, so the angler can stand in it. When netting a trout from a drifting boat, always bring the fish to the net on the windward side of the boat, to avoid drifting over the fish.

FLY FISHING ON RIVERS

STEALTH

Work your way upstream, so that you are approaching the fish from behind (trout always face upstream) and so any vibrations from clumsy footsteps will tend to be carried downstream. Always move quietly and keep low – stealth is the name of the game.

WHICH FLY?

Trout living in wild streams are seldom fussy about what they eat. Any fly, beetle, or caterpillar that falls on the water is eagerly grabbed. Hackled wet flies are the best kind to use when casting upstream because the soft hackles move enticingly with the current coming from behind. Winged wet flies are better for fishing downstream.

Sometimes only smaller fish will show any interest in a fly. A weighted nymph cast into the head of a pool will often tempt the deeper-lying larger fish.

Fishing on a winding stream is skillful sport. It demands great casting accuracy, although long casts are seldom required. You'll also need to master the side cast for casting where trees hang over the water. The principles are the same as the overhead cast – just lay the rod over and cast parallel to the water. In any event, always look behind you before casting to see if there are any obstructions which may snag you on the back cast.

You'll need only a small selection of flies. For dry flies try a general insect imitation, such as March Brown, in sizes 16, 14, and 12. Your wet flies need only include a general imitation in sizes 16, 14, and 12, and perhaps a couple of sizes in a fat beetle pattern. A few size 14 or 12 weighted nymphs may also come in handy. Although some flies look nothing like a natural insect, you will find they work surprisingly well.

March Brown

Cardinal

specific black fly imitation

general insect imitation

beetle imitation

Twinkle Orange (weighted nymph)

WHICH FISH?

If you see several fish rising in the same pool, cast to the best one. Small trout tend to make splashy rises in more open water, moving around as they do so. Larger trout seldom make much disturbance, and are difficult to spot as they rise in the shadow of over-hanging foliage. They will usually be in a choice position, with a constant supply of insects carried on the current, and will rise in exactly the same spot time after time. If you spot a group of larger fish, cast to the downstream one first.

When you hook a fish, try not to let it run up the pool, where it may spook other feeding fish. On a small, rough stream, some strong handling will be required to keep a large trout clear of snags. In this sort of situation, using too fine a tippet on your leader is asking for trouble – use no finer than 3 lb, or 4 lb if the stream is particularly snaggy.

PRESENTING A DRY FLY DOWNSTREAM

Where the banks are overgrown, you might have to cast downstream. The casting is not itself a problem, but it may be difficult to keep the fly from being dragged across the surface in an unnatural manner.

When casting to a fish that is downstream of you, make the fly fall just upstream of the fish. Attempt to introduce some slack as the line lands on the water.

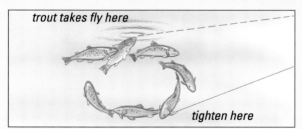

Wait until the trout has turned well down with the fly before setting the hook.

PRESENTING THE FLY

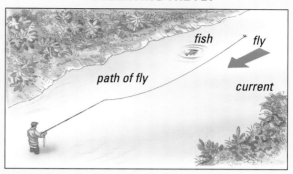

Cast your fly just upstream of a rising fish and allow it to float naturally downstream. Keep in touch with the fly by collecting slack line with your free hand, retrieving the line at the same speed as the current.

Wait until the fish has turned down with the fly before setting the hook. If the fish rises to your fly but you fail to hook it, pause to see if it keeps on feeding. If it does not you have probably made it nervous, and it is time to cast to the next fish upstream.

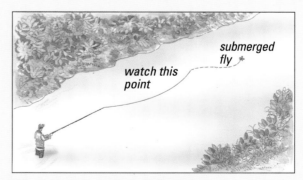

When you present a wet fly or a nymph, watch the end of the line and tighten to any suspicious movement. Quite often the fish will hook itself, especially in fast-running water.

SALTWATER FLY FISHING

The use of fly-type lures in conjunction with a fly rod and reel is a relatively new form of sea fishing, with the "flies" imitating not insects but small fish, prawns, or squid. It is practiced mainly in the warmer waters of North America, South Africa, and Australia for fish such as barracuda, bonefish, and tarpon. However, it also works in colder waters – bass, mackerel, and sea trout can all be caught on fly-fishing gear.

TACKLE
A No. 8/9 rod, 9-10 ft in length, with a fairly stiff action, is the ideal weapon for shore and boat work. The reel must be strong with a wide spool, loaded with as much backing line as it will comfortably accommodate. You'll need reels with sinking as well as floating lines available, so you can vary the depth of the retrieve. Braided leaders are best, and tippets should be 6- to 10-lb monofilament.

This reel is ideal for saltwater fly fishing. It will hold plenty of strong line and backing. It is made of non-rusting material and can cope with fast-running fish.

FISHING THE FLY
A spell of warm settled weather, with little or no wind, provides the ideal conditions for fly fishing for bass or mackerel as they feed on sandeels just off shore. Feeding activity is usually signaled by diving gulls and terns. Approach the area by boat, cutting the motor before you fish.

Bass and mackerel feeding in this manner will often be right on the surface, but the best specimens are usually swimming deeper, waiting for any dead or wounded fry to sink into their waiting jaws. A white and silver fly, tied to a 1/0 or 2/0 hook, will give a good impression of darting silver sandeels.

This huge fly is used for tarpon, a strong, skillful game fish that can weigh as much as 200 lbs.

Saltwater lures, such as these for bonefish, are often made using reflective materials such as Mylar and Flashabou.

Fish will often nose at fragments of weed, so a lure resembling seaweed might be their undoing. Try the silver-bodied Alexandra, which has green peacock feathers and a red tail as an added attraction. It was originally designed for sea trout, which often move upstream with mullet.

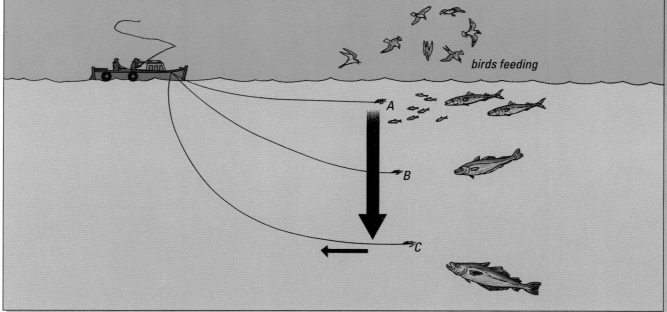

RETRIEVING

Where predatory fish are feeding near the surface, retrieve the fly just beneath the surface (A). Alternatively, let the fly sink (imitating a wounded or dead fry) – possibly catching a fish on-the-drop (B) – followed by a deep retrieve hoping to make contact with a deep-lying larger fish (C).

birds feeding

A

B

C

Some enormous fish can be caught on fly rods and reels – such as this magnificent sailfish. The sailfish stuns its prey with its "beak" before eating them.

ESTUARIES

A narrow estuary mouth is a favorite haunt of bass. Cast across the current with a sinking line, retrieving the fly at a fairly rapid pace – and be prepared for the solid resistance of a hooked bass! You can try for mullet over shallow water farther up the estuary, perhaps using a floating line so the fly doesn't snag the bottom.

ANGLER'S HINT
When fishing from rocks into deeper water, try to fish at different depths to find where the most fish are feeding.

INDEX

Italic figures refer to captions or to illustration labels.

angling clubs 9, 16

backing line 64
bait 8, *16*, *19*, *24*, 34-37
  fly fishing *69*
  sea fishing *55*, 56, *59*, 62-63
  wobbled 48
bass 50, 54, 56-58, 60, *62-63*, 75
beads *39*
billy *61*
bite indicator 41, 46, 69
  see also strike indicator
bites 28-29
boat fishing 58-61
  fly fishing *71*
bobbin indicator 41, 46
bodied floats 27
bonefish *74*
brandlings *37*
bread 34, *35*, 39, 44, *59*
bream *37*
butt indicator 41

carp 10, 32, *34*, *35*, 37
casting 18-19, 45, 53, 67
cheese *37*
chub *34*, 35
clamworm *62*
clothing *15*, 52
cod 53, *55*, 60, *62*
code of conduct 9
cork ball floats *26*
crabs *62*
crosswinds 19

dabs *62*
deadbait 48, 49
disgorger *14*, 28, *33*
dogfish 60

egg floats *26*
elastic tip 43
electrical wires 17
equipment 8
estuaries *29*, 55, 56, 75

feeders 40
flick tip 43
flies, artificial 65, 70-71, 72, *73*, *74*
float 16, *25*, 26, 27, 28
  deadbait 48, *49*
  pole *43*
float fishing 8, *17*
  casting 18
  rivers 24-27
  shore *57*
  still water 20-23
floatant 71
flounders 53, *55*, 56, 58-59, *62*
fly fishing 8, 64-73
  saltwater 74-75
fly line 64, 66

groundbait 36, 40

handling fish 8, 32-33
harbors 54, 56
hooks 12, 28, 53

jetties 54, *56*

keepnet *14*, *16*, *17*, *32*
knots 13, 64

landing 30-33, 45
landing net *14*, *16*, 32, 46
  sea fishing 56, 58, 61
leaders 12, 66
license 16
line 12, 26, 52, 64, *66*
lugworms *62*
lunch meat *37*, 39

lure fishing weights 50
lures *16*, 50, 58, *61*
  fly fishing 65, 70, *74*

mackerel 56, 58, *60*, *63*
maggots *34*, 44
midges *69*
"monkey climb" indicator 46
mullet 75

night crawlers *37*
nymphs 65, 68, *69*, 72, *73*

offshore boat fishing 60-61
Olivette weights 44

perch *37*, 46, 50
permit 16
pike 10, 29, 32, 33, 46, 48, 50, *51*
plastic bubble floats *25*, *26*
playing the fish 8, 30, *31*
plugs *28*, 50-51
plumbing the depth 20
plummet 20
pole fishing 8, 42-45
pole rigs 44, *45*
pollack 60
prawns *63*
predators 8, *28*, 46-49, 75

quill floats *20*, *21*
quivertips 41

recordkeeping 23, 32
redworms *37*
reel 10, 16, 24, 46, 52
  care 10
  drag 17
  fly-fishing 64, *65*, *66*, 74
  loading *11*
  spin-casting *9*, 11
  spinning *9*, 11
retrieve 51, 68 75
rivers, fly-fishing 72-73
rod action 11
rod rest *14*, *15*, 46, *54*
rods 10, 16, 50, *51*, 52
  fly fishing 64
  offshore boat fishing 61
rubber squid *61*

safety 9, 17, 52, 58
sailfish 75
sandeel lures *61*

sea fishing 8, 52-3
  bait 62-3
  fly fishing 74-75
seat box *15*
setting the hook 28, 29, 73
setting up 16
shock leader 52
shore fishing 8, 54-57
  rigs 55
shot 21, 22
sinkers *38*, *39*
sleeves *43*, *45*
snags 27, 57
snaps *38*, 50
spin-casting reels *9*, *11*, 25
spinners *28*, 50-51
spinning reels *9*, *11*, 24
spinning rods 50
spools 12
spoons 50-51, *58*
spring balance *15*
squid *63*
stick floats 26, *27*
stillwater rigs 21
styl weights 44
surfcasting rod *52*, 56
swingtips 41
swivels *38*, 50

tackle 9, 12, *38-41*
  box *14*, *16*
tarpon *74*
tides 52
trout 46, 50, *65*, 68, *69*, 71-73
turbot 60

umbrella *15*
unhooking 32, *33*

walleye *28*
weaver fish *57*
weights 16, *55*
  lure fishing 50
  pole fishing 44
whiting *55*, 60, *62*
wire leaders 46, 47, 50
wobbled bait 48

RED DRUM
Length 15–30 inches, 3–10 pounds
Found along the Atlantic and Gulf coasts, small red drums will swim into estuaries and harbors. Larger specimens can be caught in the surf. They are partial to soft pieces of crab.

ATLANTIC CROAKER
Length 9–18 inches, ¾–4 pounds
The bottom-feeding croaker can be caught over a sandy or mud seabed in bays, the lower reaches of estuaries, and in the surf. They can be caught on a wide variety of baits.

SPOT
Length 5–15 inches, ½–2 pounds
Fairly common in Atlantic bays and coves, the spot often swims in large schools, so many can be caught in just a few minutes. Try fish, squid, or crab pieces.

WHITE SEA BASS
Length 12–48 inches, 2–15 pounds
This cousin of the drum can be caught along the Pacific coast, particularly around kelp beds. It can be caught with a wide range of methods and baits.

BLACK SEA BASS
Length 6–18 inches, ½–3 pounds
The black sea bass can be found in both inshore and offshore waters around wrecks or other obstructions. Try small pieces of sea worms, fish, or squid to tempt this beautifully colored fish.

STRIPED BASS
Length 12–40 inches, 4–20 pounds
The striped bass is found in mid-Atlantic waters. It is a powerful fighter that can be caught on both natural and artificial baits.

SPOTTED SEA TROUT
Length 15–24 inches, ¾–5 pounds
The spotted sea trout, a cousin of the northern weakfish, can be caught on various lures and baits. They are particularly partial to shrimps.

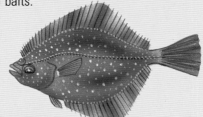

STARRY FLOUNDER
Length 8–36 inches, 1–6 pounds
The starry flounder, a flatfish, is popular with anglers along the Pacific coast. Most flatfish feed on the bottom, so use enough weight to hold your bait on the seabed.

WINTER FLOUNDER
Length 8–21 inches, ½–3 pounds
The winter flounder is the most common flounder found in shallow coastal waters. It can be caught on clams, mussels, and sandworms.

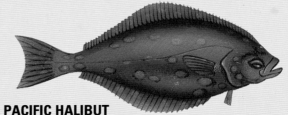

PACIFIC HALIBUT
Length 18–100 inches, 2–100 pounds
The Pacific halibut, like its cousin the Atlantic halibut, is a mainly deep-water fish that is caught on long lines from large offshore boats. A mature female can weigh 500 pounds!